Praise for

A HOLE IN THE WORLD

"Blending history with memoir, social worker Opelt examines death rituals and reflects on her season of grief in this devastating debut... Poignant and erudite, this is not to be missed."

—*Publishers Weekly* (starred review)

"A beautiful, necessary book that resounds with openhearted curiosity and gorgeous vulnerability... In exploring how others have grieved, she walks us winsomely toward honesty, healing, and above all, hope."

—Jeff Chu, co-author, with Rachel Held Evans, of the *New York Times* bestseller *Wholehearted Faith*

"With compelling personal narrative alongside theological, historical, and cultural inquiry, Amanda Held Opelt... invites us to put our aching bodies in motion, to glimpse at the surviving we can all do. Because grief, like love, like hope, is a learning. It does not return us to the before. The learning of grief does, however, enliven the after—and I suppose we'd call that resurrection."

—Jen Pollock Michel, author of *In Good Time* and *A Habit Called Faith*

"A HOLE IN THE WORLD is a wonderfully conceived and beautifully written book...It is, in part, an anthropology of grieving, a powerful memoir, and glimpses into a heartbreaking diary. In a world where rituals of grief are slowly vanishing, it reintroduces us to some of the most creative forms from Western culture. Most of the time the book is looking back on the rich history of rituals of pain, from cards to casseroles, from wearing black to sitting shiva. But it also looks forward, preparing our hearts for what will inevitably happen to us all."

—Michael Card, songwriter and
author of *A Sacred Sorrow*

"A HOLE IN THE WORLD is both generous and generative, a book that tenderly guides us into the fierce landscape of our own losses, because the author has dared to walk there first. Few of us today know how to speak of our sorrows, but in this book Held Opelt gives us language for loss that is honest, hopeful, and gorgeously human."

—K. J. Ramsey, licensed professional counselor and
author of *This Too Shall Last* and
The Lord Is My Courage

A HOLE IN THE WORLD

FINDING HOPE IN RITUALS OF GRIEF AND HEALING

AMANDA HELD OPELT

New York • Nashville

Worthy Books
Hachette Book Group
1290 Avenue of the Americas, New York, NY 10104
worthypublishing.com
twitter.com/worthypub

First Trade Edition: July 2023
Originally published in hardcover and ebook by Worthy in July 2022.

Worthy Books is a division of Hachette Book Group, Inc.

The Worthy Books name and logo are trademarks of Hachette Book Group, Inc.

The publisher is not responsible for websites (or their content) that are not owned by the publisher.

The Hachette Speakers Bureau provides a wide range of authors for speaking events. To find out more, go to hachettespeakersbureau.com or email HachetteSpeakers@hbgusa.com.

Worthy Books may be purchased in bulk for business, educational, or promotional use. For information, please contact your local bookseller or the Hachette Book Group Special Markets Department at special.markets@hbgusa.com.

Library of Congress Cataloging-in-Publication Data
Names: Opelt, Amanda Held, author.
Title: A hole in the world : finding hope in rituals of grief and healing / Amanda Held Opelt.
Description: First edition. | New York : Worthy, 2022. | Includes bibliographical references.
Identifiers: LCCN 2021059697 | ISBN 9781546001898 (hardcover) | ISBN
  9781546001911 (ebook)
Subjects: LCSH: Bereavement—Religious aspects. | Grief—Religious aspects.
Classification: LCC BL65.B47 O64 2022 | DDC 204/.42—dc23/eng20220314
LC record available at https://lccn.loc.gov/2021059697

ISBN: 9781546001904 (trade pbk.), 9781546001911 (ebook)

Printed in the United States of America
LSC-C
Printing 1, 2023

For Mom and Dad
And in loving memory of Rachel

"Where you used to be,
there is a hole in the world,
which I find myself constantly
walking around in the daytime,
and falling in at night."

—

Edna St. Vincent Millay

CONTENTS

A
HOLE
IN THE
WORLD

ASH WEDNESDAY

It is high noon on Ash Wednesday and I am lost in the church basement.

I had shown up fashionably late to the midday service. I frantically navigated my car to one of the few remaining spaces and ran across the parking lot, the echo of my heels bouncing off the brick walls of the church. I made my way toward the first door I happened to see on the west side of the building. Incidentally, this was the door to the basement, not the sanctuary, so while the rest of the penitents at St. Luke's Episcopal Church in downtown Boone, North Carolina, were bathed in stained glass–filtered sunlight, I was stuck halfway underground, deciphering my way through dark, flannelgraph-lined hallways, a musty-smelling rec center, and mazes of makeshift offices.

Considering the year I'd had, the metaphor is not lost on me. Fortunately, I hear the clinking of a teacup and find a woman in a small kitchen—she may have been on staff or a volunteer. I explain that this isn't my home church, that I am lost, and that I need help getting to the sanctuary. She points past a foosball table to a heavy wooden door that leads to a staircase that leads to a foyer that leads to the sanctuary. I rush up the stairs full speed ahead, my heavy, water-resistant winter coat swooshing with every hurried step.

Inconveniently, the sanctuary is arranged in such a way that the main doors enter at the front by the altar. Clearly the building's architect had never been late to church. Breathing heavily as I approach the entrance, I am faced with a decision. Do I give up the whole endeavor, trudge back to my car, and resolve to be more prompt in the future? Or do I burst through the doors in the midst of the silent reflection, a spectacle of irreverence?

Fortunately, I am not alone in my tardiness. A young, bearded Boone hipster, clad in a large trench coat, appears with the same quickened breath and panicked look on his face. We make eye contact, shrug at each other, and proceed toward the door. Grabbing a copy of the liturgy, I wait for him to enter first. I figure if I can draft behind him, maybe his broad trench coat will conceal me. No one will see me. I will make myself small. I will not be exposed.

We tiptoe in, dodging the priests' stares, and make our way to the back rows. There I sit, in the last pew, wondering if I've remembered to turn off my cell phone, but too scared to reach over to check it on account of my swooshing coat. I should have worn my fleece pullover. I am as still as a statue. The room is utterly silent save for the occasional creaking of the wooden beams above us.

Be still, Amanda. Be still.

The liturgy starts:

> Return to the LORD, your God,
>   for he is gracious and merciful,
> slow to anger, and abounding in steadfast love,
>   and relents from punishing.
> Who knows whether he will not turn and relent,
>   and leave a blessing behind him. (Joel 2:13–14 NRSVA)

Bless. Blessing. Blessed. A word that endeavors to hold the mystery of the goodness of God, now reduced to a hashtag highlighting our veneers of happiness: the Pinterest-worthy house, the Instagrammable vacation, the picture-perfect marriage.

The priest continues:

> "And, to make a right beginning of repentance, and as a
> mark of our mortal nature, let us now kneel before the
> Lord, our Maker and Redeemer."

I take a deep breath. Ash Wednesday was an important day for my sister. That is the reason I am here at Saint Luke's, observing this holy day and participating in this unfamiliar ritual. She and I grew up in a loving Christian home with parents who modeled a faith infused with grace and inquisitiveness. Because we lived in the South, we were immersed in the evangelical subculture of the Bible Belt, and in her early twenties, my sister began to question many of the theological aspects of that subculture. Through the fear and disorientation of that experience, she found an anchor in the ancient liturgy of the High Church. The time-honored recitations grounded her and calmed her doubts. They provided a next right step when she didn't know how to move forward. She'd become Episcopalian in recent years, but she belonged to many faith traditions. Evangelicals, Orthodox, Catholics, and atheists alike embraced her story of faithful wrestling with the truth and stubborn insistence that all are welcome at the table of Christ.

It was this tumultuous journey of faith that led her to begin writing a blog almost fifteen years ago, which quickly gained a worldwide following. Spiritual sojourners and the religiously marginalized flocked to her website and speaking engagements, finding companionship in her thoughtful reflections, wry sense of humor, curious engagement with Scripture, and compassionate embrace of the broken and wounded in the world. She went on to write five books, several of which made it on the *New York Times* best-seller list. Thousands followed her lead, dismantling many of the dogmatic religious systems that come with cultural Christianity, but finding Jesus again, like she did, somewhere along the way. My sister, Rachel Held Evans, was a once-in-a-generation writer, a prophetic voice in the wilderness, a lover of Christ, and the forerunner of a movement.

She'd written a blog post on Ash Wednesday in 2019, one year before my tardy appearance at the St. Luke's service. In the blog she stated how she would provide resources throughout Lent for confession and reflection on her website and via posts on social media. It was the last blog she ever wrote, and many of the posts she promised were never to be. Because my perfectly healthy thirty-seven-year-old sister contracted the flu a few weeks after writing that blog. She struggled to recover, went to the hospital, began experiencing static brain seizures, and died.

To write it even now seems like an act of betrayal to her. To write it is to accept it, to name it as true, to admit the impossible. She had a three-year-old son and an eleven-month-old daughter. How could this have happened? How could God have let this happen?

"...Who knows whether he will not turn and relent..."

I fumble with my copy of the liturgy and Book of Common Prayer. My husband, Tim, and I are decidedly a nondenominational kind of people. My hands and mouth are unaccustomed to these formal incantations. Contemporary praise and worship are my mother tongue. But it has been a year of learning new languages.

"Almighty God, you have created us out of the dust of the earth: Grant that these ashes may be to us a sign of our mortality and penitence, that we may remember that it is only by your gracious gift that we are given everlasting life; through Jesus Christ our Savior. Amen."

I take another deep breath. Five days before the Ash Wednesday service, I'd taken a pregnancy test that came back positive. Due to a miscarriage back in December, the doctor wanted to monitor me closely, ordering several blood tests to evaluate my hormone levels. The blood tests revealed that the situation was bleak. The levels were low, were not rising the way they should in a healthy pregnancy.

I'd spent the early part of the week anxiously searching Doctor Google for any sign of hope, finding the rare exceptions of mothers whose hormone levels started low but went on to have perfectly healthy pregnancies. But my body had been here before. I'd lost two other babies—had experienced the halting of a heartbeat within my womb. I knew what it was to carry death in my body, to say goodbye to someone who was a part of me but whom I never really knew.

I had awoken on Ash Wednesday morning knowing, but stubbornly refusing to admit, that it was over. Over before it began. "Remember that you are dust, and to dust you shall return."

It is time for the ashes. I awkwardly approach the front, taking my cues from the more experienced Episcopalians around me. I don't want to mess up, don't want to look like a novice. But this is new to me. This is all new to me. I don't know how to carry death. The burden is still strange to me and I am clumsy in the bearing of it.

The priest reaches down and smudges my forehead with ashes, the mark of my mortal nature. My bangs get in the way and when I brush them aside, tiny flecks of ash start raining down on my nose. I avoid eye contact. My coat swooshes loudly as I return to my pew. "Remember that you are dust, and to dust you shall return."

I stare at the back of the trench-coat hipster's head. There are songs during the service, a homily, more moments of reflection. I struggle to focus on the liturgy. It's painful to focus. My mind ping-pongs between the fearsome nature of existence and the mundane particulars of living in this world. I am going to die. I wonder what we should have for dinner tonight. Someday my body will be rotting in the ground. Did Tim remember to put gas in the car? Tim will be worm food one day. Have I been to the dentist yet this year? Is God mad at me? How long will it be before I start bleeding?

Before Jesus drank the cup of sorrow and iniquity, He took a different cup with His disciples. He drank wine and broke bread with them. In this commonplace act of sharing a meal, He demonstrated divinely existential love. We take the elements as well, this repentant noonday crowd at St. Luke's on Ash Wednesday. Our foreheads smeared with our mortality, we proceed once more to the altar, extending clammy, grateful hands to receive the bread. We drink from a communal cup. It tastes of grace and mercy.

We cannot know that in a few short weeks, a global pandemic would shut down the entire world. Public gatherings and the sharing of the cup would become dangerous, and we'd spend the months to follow huddled in our houses desperately trying to slow the spread of death. The Ash Wednesday service was one of the last large group gatherings I attended in 2020. It was one of the last times I reached out my hands to physically pass the peace and feel the touch of a stranger. I failed to savor it, to bask in the beauty of shared worship. We simply have no idea what is coming.

> Deliver me from death, O God,
> and my tongue shall sing of your righteousness,
> O God of my salvation.
> Open my lips, O Lord,
> and my mouth shall proclaim your praise.[1]

As the service concludes, I wonder if anyone even remembers I'd been late. It seems a small transgression in the grand scheme of things. "Peace be with you," the priest says. We reply: "And also with you." We are encouraged to leave in silence. We exit to the sound of swooshing coats and clacking heels. We go out into the world wearing on our foreheads what we know in the marrow: we are all going to die.

I start bleeding the next morning.

• • • • •

This is a book about sorrow. It is not written in stages. It does not resolve or make precise recommendations. It meanders, as sadness so often does, through unresolved reflections and feelings: confusion, desperation, determination, hope.

I've suffered through a season of loss. In November 2016, my grandmother passed away while I was in East Africa for a work trip, and I was unable to make it home in time for the funeral. In January 2017, I traveled to work as a staff chaplain in a combat hospital just outside Mosul, Iraq. I saw with my own eyes what war can do to bodies and souls. The following July, I had a miscarriage after years of struggling with infertility. I went on to give birth to a healthy baby girl a little over a year later, but it was during her eighth month of life that my sister got sick and passed away. At Christmastime after my sister's death, I learned I was pregnant again and we quietly rejoiced that the awful and unimaginable year might end on a high note. A few days before Christmas, as I was enduring my first holiday season without my sister, I learned during a routine doctor's visit that my baby's heart had stopped beating. Two months later, it was Ash Wednesday. I was miraculously pregnant again, but not for long.

I've tried hard to steel myself in the face of all this loss. I've tried to manage people's perceptions of me, determined to be the resilient humanitarian aid worker, the dutiful sister, the heartbroken but hopeful mother-not-yet-to-be. In doing so, I often neglected the significant toll all this sorrow had taken on me. I'd spend my days denying my own brokenness, circling the sorrow, unwilling to truly approach it. Then, I'd spend my evenings in fits of weepy rage, despairing and wondering why I felt like I was going crazy.

• • • • •

As I write this, the worldwide death toll from COVID-19 has surpassed five million. Hundreds of thousands have died in the United States alone and the number is growing daily. Hospitals are at capacity, morgues in some regions are full, and lockdowns and social distancing protocols continue. The economic impact has led to global food shortages and financial instability. Scientists raced to roll out a miraculous vaccine, but variants continue to emerge and large segments of our population remain vulnerable. Under-developed nations and remote regions of the world lack access to the vaccine and to effective treatments. We have no idea how many more will die and people live with the constant, foreboding dread that the virus is coming for them and their family next. The fear and uncertainty are palpable.

All of us have been touched by this pandemic. The threat of death to ourselves and the ones we love has impacted every area of our lives. For the time being, we are cognitively tethered to our mortality in a way we haven't been for decades.

Just before the pandemic began, I came across an article about historic grief rituals from across the world. Many of the rituals from non-Western cultures are still practiced today. But most that were rooted in Western societies have died out, lost to cultural amalgamation and modernization. This article sparked my interest and started me on a journey of exploring the history of grief.

These solemn practices surrounding mourning intrigued me because I felt a distinct lack of ritual in my life in the aftermath of my losses. I'd spent the day of my grandmother's funeral in meetings at an aid worker compound in Congo. Two of my pregnancy losses were managed surgically. I'd gone into outpatient surgery as a woman *with* child and had come out a few short, anesthetized hours later *without* child. The weeks that had followed my sister's death were a flurry of funeral planning, taking care of kids, and driving back and forth between my home and hers. The tasks, to-do lists, and trivialities of life had taken over my grieving process. As crude as the metaphor is, it was like I was lost in the basement with foosball and flannelgraph when what I needed was a sanctuary with ashes and holy water.

During the course of my study, I discovered that generations past had a robust array of rituals surrounding death that allowed mourners to be fully present in the *experience* of bereavement. These customs and traditions carved out a path and led the mourner through the physical, emotional, and spiritual exercises of saying goodbye.

We are a world that is slowly losing rituals. As religious practice declines and globalization dilutes cultures, customs surrounding birth, aging, marriage, and death are being forgotten. American evangelicals in particular have sometimes cultivated a skepticism toward rituals. Many of the sacraments and formalities of the High Church are seen as impersonal, empty, and mechanically habitual. Evangelicalism has, by and large, exchanged the supposed rote redundancy of shared liturgy for the individualized freedom of contemporary praise and worship. We default to personalized spiritual growth plans rather than scripted communal ceremonies.

Western society at large has developed a deep aversion to pain. We are experts at numbing hurt, drugging discomfort, and palliating narratives that offend our sense of comfort or safety. We speak in euphemisms. We *think* in euphemisms. We put our best face forward on social media. We avoid silence and boredom at all costs, fearful that the quiet and stillness might force us to confront our own hurts and emptiness.

These days, medical facilities and funeral homes perform the few remaining grief rituals for us with sanitized efficiency. Customs surrounding death have been outsourced from the home to the hospital, from neighbors to strangers, from kinsmen to "professionals." Funeral services are relatively brief, and one is implicitly expected to return to normal life within a few short weeks of the loss. If we don't feel okay, we pretend.

The self-help industry has convinced us that we can "life-hack" our way to ease and blessedness. If we are self-care savvy and adequately mindful, then we can circumvent any of life's inconveniences and promptly experience well-being. We are optimizers to the core, absorbing bite-size therapeutic aphorisms via Instagram as we stand in line at the grocery store or wait in traffic. If there's a shortcut available, we'll take it. If there's a speedy solution, we're sold.

But there is no life hack for grief.

In school, I was taught reading, writing, and dubious amounts of extraneous arithmetic. I was taught home economics and history, music and microbiology. I learned to play volleyball and how to keep time in the marching band. In Sunday school I learned the sinner's prayer and the Ten Commandments. I memorized the names of all the books of the Bible in order and could recite countless Scripture passages. At my Christian college, I learned about the spiritual disciplines and was introduced to systematic theology.

I learned to serve, to pray, to worship, to study, and to love. But I never learned how to lose someone. I never learned how to grieve.

The ability to grieve deeply is a survival skill, one we've come close to losing as a society. The only way to experience sorrow is to do so wholeheartedly. With death and upheaval now surrounding us, we must recover this competency both collectively and individually if we are to emerge from this season whole and intact. We need to reclaim our traditions. We need to rediscover our rituals.

In the pages that follow, I will explore twelve rituals of bereavement. While some of the rituals are still in use to this day, few are mainstream, and most have died out or are practiced by only small pockets of society. Most of the rituals I've selected are rooted in Western culture or in Abrahamic faith traditions. I've chosen them not to neglect the scores of beautiful bereavement customs from around the world and within other faith traditions, but because I wanted to explore the rituals that my *own* culture had lost and to perhaps understand why we had lost them.

I don't make any promises with this book. I can't provide a to-do list that, if followed, will magically resurrect some forgotten rite of passage into healing. This isn't a DIY ritual renovation project. It's not a five-step plan for bypassing your sorrow through sanctimonious ceremony.

Frankly, some of these historic habits edge close enough to the bizarre that they would be nearly impossible to replicate in our current context. In many cases, the origin stories and historical significance of the customs are lost to the past, adding to their mystery and strangeness. Author and historian Colin Dickey said it well: "Our inability to trace the origins and meanings of such mourning rituals suggests that we sometimes carry out practices whose meaning we do not know and could not hope to know or to understand. It is often the physical act of the ritual itself, more than any possible meaning behind it, which matters. The ritual act itself is something of an empty vessel: it holds whatever we put into it, means what we want it to mean."[2]

What I do hope to uncover are the emotional longings that were met by some of these curious practices. What was the felt need beneath the ritual, and if the ritual is gone, what, if anything, is meeting that need now? When we abandoned our rituals, we left a gaping hole in our experience of grief. In our rush to arrive at the hoped-for destination, we forgot the journey and lost our way.

In my hour of grief, rituals found me. They became signposts for me along the difficult path I was walking. Rituals helped me realize that I was not alone, and I was not lost. I was simply on a journey in a strange, new land.

A ritual is not magic. Like the Ash Wednesday liturgy, it simply ushers us into the reality of our own mortality and aids in the acclimation to a significant loss. I picture rituals like smooth stones stretched across a rushing river. They provide the next right step across the torrent and set our bodies in motion. I needed an empty vessel for my grief. I needed time-honored traditions and tested rituals. I needed a next right step.

CHAPTER 1

KEENING

(ANGUISH)

Now, you women, hear the word of the Lord;
open your ears to the words of his mouth.
Teach your daughters how to wail;
teach one another a lament.
Death has climbed in through our windows.
—Jeremiah 9:20–21

Annie Dillard once wrote, "Mountains are giant, restful, absorbent. You can heave your spirit into a mountain and the mountain will keep it, folded, and not throw it back."[1]

I love living in the mountains. I feel safe here in the Blue Ridge of southern Appalachia, tucked in and sheltered. The mountains loom large over my fears and doubts, lending their perspective and timelessness. These hills are especially old, some say the oldest in the world. There is something deeply consoling in knowing that the landscape around me was carved out over many millennia by terrestrial upheaval, glacial forces, and the erosion of incessant ice and water. Their history is one of resilience and resolve, forged by the chisel of God.

There is no tumult these hills have not known. And yet, unlike other mountain ranges, whose peaks and pinnacles stand as proud edifices, grand and uninviting, the Appalachians have a humble, habitable quality to them, like you could make your home in them and not be swallowed up. These are hills that have settled into themselves. Having matured beyond the desire to intimidate, they are obliging and hospitable in nature.

When I was a little girl growing up in Birmingham, my family and I would often make the long drive up through the foothills of northern Alabama and East Tennessee so that we could visit my great-grandmother Grace Burleson, who lived in Bakersville, North Carolina, a tiny mountain town in the shadow of Roan Mountain.

The Roan Highlands are a long ridge of grassy balds and spruce-covered knobs stretching along the border of Tennessee and North Carolina. Some say this section of mountains is the prettiest in all of Appalachia. Since the 1800s, my ancestors have been trekking up the side of Roan Mountain in the springtime so they could witness the pale pink blooming of the rhododendrons. They went on foot, hiking up back country trails, tugging mules loaded down with bedding and food supplies behind them. In the 1980s, my family was fortunate enough to have a Chevy Caprice and a smooth two-lane highway that took us directly up to Roan High Knob, the highest point in the Roan Highlands, reaching over six thousand feet in elevation.

Inevitably, every time we made the journey, we were met by a wall of clouds. Old-timers in the area used to say that the Roan creates its own weather, that you can be bathed in full sunlight down in Bakersville and get drenched in a downpour up on the balds. My sister, Rachel, and I didn't mind. We were city girls from the flatlands, entranced by the mystery and majesty of the mountains. We would pile out of the Chevy into the dense fog, eager and shivering. Rachel would immediately take off running at full speed into the wall of white while I, more reticent, would move cautiously into the obscured mountain clime, tiptoeing at first, and then bounding after her. I can see it with crystal clarity even now, as if it were only yesterday: Rachel leaping in long strides, her arms outstretched and ponytail whipping in the wind behind her. She is moving in and out of sight, appearing and disappearing behind the mist. "Look, Amanda!" she squeals. "I'm flying! I'm flying through the clouds!"

I still go up to the Roan, more often now that I live only an hour away. Shortly after Rachel's funeral, I requested a leave of absence from work, and I spent the first day of my leave driving the winding roads over to Bakersville and up to the Roan. As my Subaru negotiated the hairpin turns, I reflected on the last two months of my life. It had all been a blur, the sudden onset of Rachel's illness, the creeping dread as she steadily grew worse, the shock of her death, and the flurry of funeral planning and caregiving for her two young children. I'd come to the Roan because I needed to heave my soul into a mighty mountain that would not give way. I needed to be hemmed in. I thought perhaps King David, who looked to the mountains even as death seemed to overshadow him, was onto something: "I lift my eyes to the mountains—where does my help come from?" (Ps. 121:1).

Even in her death, Rachel and I played the roles we always had, she the pioneer and pathfinder, I the deferential follower. Intrepid and inquisitive, Rachel let her heart lead her a million miles down any road she deemed worth following. I, on the other hand, had spent my life idolizing her audacity. I would often overthink things and was driven by duty rather than ideals. I was the steady one, levelheaded and practical. If Rachel was Mary, I was Martha. She was passionate and I was prudent. Though loyal and loving, Rachel never asked anyone's permission to break boundaries and step into the unknown. I was often irked by my own timidity. I was private, measured, and controlled.

It was not a fate she'd asked for, but I am certain Rachel confronted death head-on and with unrelenting fortitude, as she did every other endeavor in her life. Left behind, I was evading grief like a meek and skittish mouse. I'd busied myself with tasks and responsibilities, the spaces I knew best. I'd come to the Roan, to a place I sensed knew me better than I knew myself, so I could gather my courage and so I could hear myself think.

Of course, it was cloudy at the top. A driving rain had left the rhododendron blossoms wilted and weighed down with water. I parked in the familiar gravel lot and stepped into a world of white mist. For a moment, her spry, childlike figure passed before my eyes. Rachel is flying through the clouds. I feel forever bound to an earth she no longer inhabits.

On my way back down the mountain, I stopped by the family cemetery, which is situated just to the northwest of the old Burleson farm and homestead. Since the early 1800s, my ancestors, including Granny Grace and my grandparents, have made this grassy knoll in the shadow of the Roan their final resting place. As the decades passed and the family expanded, the headstones have crept closer and closer to the tree line. There are very few spaces remaining, and I am told if you want to be buried in the graveyard, you need to reserve your spot *now*.

The gate was rusted out and heavy to move, but I shoved it with all my strength. As I stepped over the headstones of my great-aunts and -uncles and second and third cousins over to where my grandparents are buried, I heard myself murmuring: "Rachel died. Grandma, Rachel got really sick. We buried her in Tennessee. Granddaddy, Rachel didn't make it. I just thought you should know."

That was as far as my language got me. Standing over the bodies of my ancestors, something inside me snapped. Suddenly, a cry erupted from my mouth that quickly broke out into a loud sob. Stumbling wildly over the crumbling headstones, and heaving the gate closed, I found my way back to my Subaru and slammed the door shut behind me. I screamed into the steering wheel. I pounded the dashboard. I shrieked over and over again. My lungs burned and my vision blurred. I wailed and wailed and wailed.

• • • • •

I am 50 percent German. My grandfathers on both my mother's side and my father's side are German; perhaps that's where I acquired my aptitude for emotional restraint. I've always had a desire to stiffly muscle through the ups and downs of life, not wanting to be or appear weak. Or, God forbid, hysterical. I want to be seen as steadfast, unflappable in the face of crisis. I like being inhibited. It makes me feel like I'm in control of how people perceive me. It makes me feel safe.

It also makes me feel holy. As a child, I was never overtly taught that emotions were bad. In fact, my parents were always insistent that matters of the heart were valid (my dad had a degree in counseling and my mom was a fourth-grade teacher, so they were wise enough to never disregard the feelings of their children, no matter how fervent or unreasonable). But I was raised in a particular brand of American evangelicalism that watched with wary eyes the impassioned and spontaneous displays of worship so common in other expressions of the church. Love for Christ in my world was best exhibited through rigorous study and commitment to a highly systematized theology. Having majored in Bible and philosophy, I was drawn to churches that prioritized expository preaching over emotive worship. If a preacher could read Greek or Hebrew, I assumed he was more spiritually mature.

Feelings were not to be trusted. They were to be controlled, constrained by facts and logic and reason. A former pastor of mine once preached from the pulpit: "God gets ahold of us through the mind and the intellect. Satan gets ahold of us through the heart and the emotions." I can see myself now, sitting in the pew, vigorously nodding my head and scribbling notes on my bulletin.

"Emotional" was a word used to describe weak or hormonal women. Or toddlers.

While my paternal roots may be German, my mother's mother was born to a family of mountain dwellers, old Appalachian stock, hardy but decidedly sentimental, ardent, whimsical, and petulant. Welsh, Scottish, Irish, French, Spanish: my mother's DNA test reveals a hodgepodge of cultures notorious not for their stoicism, but for their passion.

Perhaps it was this Irish, maternal thread that stitched a proficiency in my genes for the wail that eventually erupted in the shadow of Roan Mountain that day. The Irish, you see, have an ancient tradition practiced after the death of a loved one known as keening. A keen, most simply put, is a funeral wail—a type of refrain that is more scream than song, more cry than chorus. The Irish are certainly not the only people group whose grief rituals have historically included the practice of wailing. Some Chinese and Jewish funerals involve professional mourners to this day. Wailing aloud at the death and burial of a loved one has always been standard in West Africa, and so this practice was carried over on the Middle Passage, persisting in the traditions of Black communities during and after the violent era of slavery in America.[2] For the Irish, keening was a mystical and powerful art form, a holy act shrouded in mystery and a ritual emerging from a conglomeration of pagan and Christian beliefs.

In the olden days of Ireland, when a person would die, a room of the house would be cleared of excess furniture and the body laid out on a table. In the room, clocks would be stopped as the family and friends of the loved one entered into a liminal space, a time outside of time, to grieve and remember the dead. The wake would begin as the community came to mourn. Traditional wakes served as a type of emotional release—drinks would be served, stories shared, and games were even played. The mourners would erupt into cheers and laughter. But the climax of the wake was when the keeners, professional funeral wailers, would begin their performance.

There was often a lead keener, in Gaelic called the *bean chaointe*. This role was almost always reserved for women. Many times, midwives served as the *bean chaointe*, women who knew well the thin divide between birth and life and death. They would usher people into the world, and they would usher them out.

The act of keening served two purposes. One was to release the grief felt deep in the hearts of the mourners into the open air. The keener gave permission for people to fall apart, to grieve with their whole bodies without feeling shame.

The other purpose was to escort the dead into the other world, to the life after life. The keen would pay tribute to the lost loved one. A keen was in many ways akin to a song, but a traditional keen was not written out or handed down for reuse because it was improvised, meant to be lovingly customized for the one who passed, and sung only once over the soul for which it was specifically composed. The keen would often begin with the *bean chaointe* singing or speaking in a low chanting voice, and then progress into a louder cry, with all the mourners joining in, some chanting, some moaning. The chorus of grief would sometimes take the shape of words about the loved one, but often language would collapse under the weight of the sorrow, erupting into wails and cries.[3]

"You left me under the star of frost," one keen recorded in the mid-1900s says. "I'll never see you again."[4]

The *bean chaointe* would accompany the dead to the gravesite, often riding on top of the coffin as it was pulled by horse and cart to the final resting place. Traditionally, she would let her long hair loose to fly in the wind as she rode, personifying the natural and unruly nature of death and grief. She was a wild and evocative creature in that moment. Some even believe that the notorious screaming banshee of Irish myth is really the spirit of a deceased *bean chaointe*, forever warning the world of pending doom and death.

Keening as a tradition began to die out in the early 1900s and has all but vanished from the Irish countryside. As modernity and industrialization swept across the island, many saw the practice as uncivilized, a tradition that belonged to a primitive past. The church banned keening, seeing the worldview surrounding the ritual as a threat to the Christian understanding of the afterlife. Some believe that male clergy felt threatened by the power and influence of the female *bean chaointe* and so sought to put a stop to the ritual. As early as 1611, Protestant and Catholic churches worked through civil authorities to abolish the "howling and crying at the burial of the dead." In 1626, Galway Corporation—a largely Catholic organization—ordered that wailing in the streets at funerals should cease, stating, "All and every corpses to be caried to his grave here in sivill and orderly fashione, according to the forme in all good places observed."[5] Nevertheless, the tradition persisted for more than four hundred years.

The *bean chaointe* embraced the sacredness of her duties, playing a role similar to counselors and therapists of our day. She created space for sorrow, shouldered loss, and aided in the processing of a new and painful reality. Many keening women felt they were following in the footsteps of Mary, the mother of Jesus, sometimes referred to as the Mother of Sorrows for the many griefs she bore during her lifetime.[6] One thirteenth-century devotion articulates the perspective of Mary as she gazed upon her crucified son:

> I was tormented by such great sorrow and sadness in death that it could not be expressed in speech...my sorrow could not be kept within me. My voice had nearly gone, but I uttered sighs of sorrow and moans of grief. I wanted to speak, but sorrow broke off the words, for a word is first conceived in the mind, then proceeds to formation by the mouth. Too great sorrow of the heart calls back the word imperfect. A sad voice sounds on the outside, declaring the wound of the mind. Love provides the words, but they sound harsh, for the tongue, the mistress of the voice, had

lost the skill of speaking. I saw him dying, whom my soul loved, and my soul was completely dissolved by the anguish of sorrow.[7]

It seems that the labor of birth and the labor of death have always been women's work.

• • • • •

I'm not sure how a person as anxious and wary as me got involved in international aid work. I suppose I came in through the back door. My first real job out of college was as a nonprofit worker in the inner city. I'd burned out doing that work and wanted to minister to others in the helping profession, coming alongside them as they built skills for resilience and longevity. I'd spent six months in India in my early twenties tutoring HIV orphans and widows, and I guess the international humanitarian bug bit me. I started my work as a staff care professional to international aid workers, thinking I knew a thing or two about suffering and trauma. I didn't realize how woefully unqualified I was.

The full weight of my incompetence hit me in January 2017, when I served as a staff chaplain at a field hospital just outside Mosul, Iraq. The military campaign by the Iraqi government and its allies to retake Mosul from ISIS control was in full swing, and our organization had set up a combat hospital to treat the wounded coming out of the city—civilians, soldiers, and suspected ISIS combatants alike.

There is nothing like seeing civilian combat wounds, particularly in women and children, to make you question everything you thought you knew about evil and suffering and loss. Daily I watched our heroic Iraqi and expatriate staff quietly wither under the weight of the responsibility of patching together broken bodies. I had no words to inspire or offer comfort. More devastatingly, I watched the trembling wounded huddle in their beds, the walls of our mobile hospital shaking as bombs rained down on their beloved city. Most had loved ones who were unaccounted for. Death was all around us.

One day an entire family was brought into the hospital after a bomb had been planted in their family car. I won't go into the graphic details of their wounds, but the mother was badly injured and clinging to life in our ICU. The youngest child, a baby, was dead. The toddler was not expected to survive. The father had suffered some superficial wounds and was admitted to the men's ward of our hospital. He had become conscious after a harrowing journey out of the city, and so it was time for me, the attending physician, and one of our Iraqi staff to meet with him and share the news of the fate of his family.

The physician, after years of serving as an ER doctor, had learned to be transparent and to the point when sharing bad news. Tenderly and concisely, she provided the status of each of his family members, one by one, through a translator. And with each piece of horrifying news, we watched the man as he descended deeper and deeper into his despair. We hovered around him and, suddenly, he released a howl from his twisting mouth that was as primal and enraged as a war cry. We watched and held his hands as his entire life crumbled around him. On the far side of the ward, under the watchful eye of guards, were suspected ISIS combatants, also wounded, looking on at the excruciating reality that their evil ideology had birthed into the world.

I've never known a more holy moment. It was as if someone had finally broken that barrier between the facade of stoic resolve required to survive this hellish reality and the true feeling deep down in our souls. His was the cry of a nation at war. His was the grief of a million fathers who have lost their children to the clutches of senseless conflict. His was the wail of a world gone mad.

To wail is, in fact, the only appropriate response to the horror of death. As writer and journalist Andrea DenHoed points out, "Mortality is never going to be a good fit…death reduces us all to hurt animals, like Lear on the heath: 'Howl, howl, howl, howl!'"[8] The death wail is unsophisticated. It is not curated. It cares not what others think of it, and it has no desire for an interpreter. It is a language meant not for communication but rather for expelling the darkness. When it breaks free, one loses all sense of propriety and performance. The wailer slips into a world of inconsequence, succumbing to the sorrow and finally expressing with unbridled veracity what is true and real about all that is being experienced: I am *destroyed*.

● ● ● ● ●

Like the modern Irish, most of us long to be sophisticated in our bereavement. It seems we are most lauded in our grief for being strong, for not allowing ourselves to be overcome. Those of us who hold up sobbing relatives, who tend to the funeral plans, who open the doors to receive the casseroles, who finish the paperwork, who plod through the eulogies without blubbering—we are affirmed for our composure, praised for our resilience.

I'd rehearsed grief in my mind a thousand times before I actually lived it. I'd practiced the performance of self-maintained righteousness, the kind that had so often won me the approval of the subculture to which I belonged. I'd cultivated a sound theology of suffering, rooting myself deeply in a systematic explanation for the anguish in the world. I'd memorized the lines I would recite in the event of a tragedy: "The Lord gives and the Lord takes away; blessed be the name of the Lord." I was certain that all my scripts and systems would bear up under the weight of whatever sorrow might come my way.

I was wholly unprepared for the reality of grief.

Most holy axioms surrounding bereavement are cruelly reductive. The death of my sister cannot be condensed into a well-rehearsed adage. The loss of my babies can't be contained in a simple cliché. The toll of war is not to be explained away by a theological system. These tragedies warrant a different category of worship, a unique rupturing of the heart before almighty God.

What I found in the breaking open was a strange and unknown holiness, like God had found some deep place inside of me that I didn't know existed. I was caught up in some swift unveiling, some harrowing of the soul. I felt as if God were saying to me, "I want you to succumb to the grief for a moment, to give yourself over to it. Don't resist. Don't fight it. Don't hide it. Just be in it. *Fully.*"

The truth is you cannot think your way out of grief. You cannot perform your way through it. There is no wellness routine or therapist that can get rid of it. You cannot pray it away. You cannot numb your feelings forever or circumvent the sorrow and go straight to the redemption.

Sometimes we have to allow grief to have its way with us for a while. We need to get lost in the landscape of grief. It is a wild and rugged wilderness terrain to be sure, but it is here that we meet our truest selves. And we are met by God. The wilderness makes no space for pretense or facade. The language of platitudes and trite niceties are of no use to us in the wilderness. In the wilderness, we speak what is primitive and primary. We say what is true. We say what is hard and heartbreaking. We wail.

It is only through this death wail, in that moment of reckoning, that we can begin our journey. We must know the landscape before we can set a course. We have to say it. We have to name it. This is going to be difficult, dangerous even. The pilgrimage of grief is a toilsome one, long and arduous. Sometimes, it lasts a lifetime.

• • • • •

"Death has climbed in through our windows." This is imagery the people of Judea would have been familiar with. The prophet Jeremiah may have been alluding to a well-known story from Canaanite mythology, in which Baal and his household suffer at the hands of Mot, the god of infertility, death, and the underworld. Baal, emboldened by his recent victory over a rival god, had built an enormous palace, unmatched in splendor and opulence. Baal's architect suggested putting windows in the palace. After initially hesitating, Baal consented, but this was his undoing because it was through the windows that Mot crept in and laid waste to the citadel.[9] Other ancient Babylonian texts speak of the demon Lamastu, who entered the homes of unsuspecting families to devour children and infants.[10]

Whether or not Jeremiah intended an overt reference to the mythologies of Israel's surrounding cultures, the image is provocative and ominous. Death is present not only in the wilderness, on the battlefields, or on the open seas. Death comes for us in our places of safety. It creeps in when we least expect it. It ascertains our vulnerabilities, presses in at the apertures. Death stalks in the night and waits for an opening, insidious and shrewd. Just when we think we are secure and sound, it strikes. We are ambushed.

In Jeremiah 9, death is part of the broader tragedy of the impending destruction of Jerusalem and the exile of the people to Babylon, a catastrophe that befalls them following their rebellion against God. It is during this era of calamity that the Lord summons the wailing women of Judea. He has a task for them, a mission fit only for those who are skilled in the rigorous art of sorrow. Verses 17 and 18 say, "Consider now! Call for the wailing women to come; send for the most skillful of them. Let them come quickly and wail over us till our eyes overflow with tears and water streams from our eyelids." Some translations refer to the women as wise or cunning.

Old Testament scholar Juliana Claassens writes that women wailers held a unique place in society, offering an invaluable gift to the community. She notes, "Trauma often leaves people numb and confused, unable to express their emotions. The wailing women's tears helped the people to break through the silence toward a basic, raw vocalization of their grief."[11] Grief was no longer hidden and private, but shared and communal. The mourners provided a space for processing and acknowledging pain together, and therefore served in an almost therapeutic role. The wailing women also acted as a witness to hurt and tragedy. They were caretakers of the memory of what was lost.

Perhaps most profoundly, the wailing women served in a prophetic role. In Jeremiah 9, their wailing is a warning. They are seers of what lies beneath the surface of our neglect and inequity. They feel and express the pain of the vulnerable, of those who will come to ruin. As Claassens writes, "The wailing women serve as God's spokespersons, as the people's conscience in protesting against the wrongs in their world."[12]

Wailing is both resistance and recognition, defiance and compliance. In the wailing, you voice your dissent while simultaneously succumbing to the havoc of your new circumstances. You beg for what once was or what you'd hoped for while also naming what has occurred and what will be. In the moaning, you reside in that liminal space between denial and acceptance. Everything is laid bare before you: the familiar past and the unexpected future.

The task of wailing is so important that in Jeremiah 9, God implores all women to teach their daughters to develop a proficiency in this honorable vocation. God calls for mothers to bequeath to their daughters the vision required of a capable condoler. The practice was so valued by the culture that it was a profession for which one was compensated, a calling that required discipline and training.

Perhaps the most heart-wrenching portion in the entire book of Jeremiah is located just a few verses before the summoning of the mourners. In these evocative verses, God steps into the role of the wailing woman:

Since my people are crushed, I am crushed; I mourn, and horror grips me. (8:21)

Oh that my head were a spring of water and my eyes a fountain of tears! I would weep day and night for the slain of my people. (9:1)

I will weep and wail for the mountains and take up a lament
concerning the wilderness grasslands. (9:10)

God. Not too proud in His glory to veil His anguish. Not so
arrogant and detached as to be unaffected by grief. Not so lofty as to
reject being associated with the perceived vulnerability of an emotional woman. In fact, it is often through vulnerability that God
shows Himself strong in love, wise and unrelenting in His grace.
Bereft of His children, He longs for reconciliation and cries out for
a different outcome. The labor of grief is not left for the wailing
women alone. Grief is God's labor.

We would all do well to apprentice ourselves to the Master
Mourner, the One who sees sorrow for what it truly is, the One
whose heart breaks for those who grieve, the One who is uninhibited in His weeping. In a world that sees the emotions of women as
a liability, let us remember that God sees them as a holy asset.

• • • • •

In spite of my theological rigor, I am a person who sometimes questions the existence of God. I wonder if we are not all merely accidents of the universe, highly developed organisms who, through
a process of natural selection, have dominated all other species.
Maybe there is no meaning. Maybe all my thoughts, feelings, and
behaviors are merely the result of a random firing of neurons in my
prefrontal cortex. Perhaps, as some have so eloquently put it, I'm
simply "the sperm that won."

The death wail says otherwise.

The death wail tells me that I am a lover. A mother. A sister. A daughter. It tells me that my relationships are more than contractual arrangements or biological associations. Divine attachments have been appointed to me. I have birthed miracles and miraculous love surrounds me. Sacred covenant tethers me to family, to community, and to God.

Love as deep as we experience daily must be divinely bestowed, a gift given to image bearers of God, a capacity belonging to beings entirely distinct from their fellow creatures. When such love is lost, the deep in us cries out to the deep in God. To wail is holy, and wholly profound.

The degree to which we mourn is an indication of the degree to which we loved. How and why would we ever reduce so great a love to suppressed sighs or proud displays of composure and fortitude? The time for strength will come. The day will arrive when we need to bravely put one foot in front of the other. There will come a moment when we will need to share stories of blessing in the midst of sorrow and lay claim to the promise of redemption and restoration.

But first, we heave our spirits into the mountain. First, we wail.

CHAPTER 2

COVERING MIRRORS

(CHANGE)

Sighing has become my daily food;
my groans pour out like water.
What I feared has come upon me;
what I dreaded has happened to me.
I have no peace, no quietness;
I have no rest, but only turmoil.
—Job 4:24-26

To know yourself is a gift.

Imagine a world where you had never seen your own face. Perhaps you had seen an obscured reflection of yourself rippling in a dark pool of water or a gentle stream. You had observed the length and width of your shadow on sunny days. But the various shades of color in your eyes were unfamiliar to you. You wouldn't know the exact contours of your face or the shape of your smile. You would be well acquainted with the faces of others, but not your own. Your self-perception would be based solely on the reactions and descriptions of those around you. You really would have no certain idea of how you *appeared* to the world.

Now imagine an object that would change all of that.

Mirrors are magical. Peer into the history of this commonplace household item, and you'll find a world of mystery. Derived from the Latin *mirare* and *mirari*, the word "mirror" means "to look at" and "to wonder at, admire." Historians believe that the first mirrors may have been invented eight thousand years ago in what is now the country of Turkey and were made of smoothed obsidian stone. Two thousand years later, the Chinese were making mirrors of polished bronze. Modern-day mirrors are made of glass, silver, and aluminum.

Over the years, mirrors have been valued for much more than their ability to reflect a person's countenance. Many cultures used them as a tool for seeing the future. The Mayans believed mirrors provided a window into the world of the gods and deceased ancestors. The Chinese believed mirrors could dispel evil spirits and bring fortune to a home.[1] To this day, breaking a mirror is seen as a bad omen.

Laborious and expensive to create, for most of human history mirrors were possessed by only the wealthy elite. It was just in the last few centuries that the average household gained access to their own images. It's hard for those of us raised in a world of compact mirrors, smartphone cameras, and social media selfies to relate to this absence of personal images. I know exactly what I look like. Perhaps too well. Self-reflective by nature, even self-obsessed, my generation may relate more to the mythological character of Narcissus, who fell in love with his own reflection in a pool of water. But imagine the moment of awe and transcendence in seeing your reflection for the very first time. It is no wonder mirrors hold such a powerful space in our minds.

For reasons historians can't precisely explain, multiple cultures have had customs and rituals surrounding mirrors in the wake of death. Traditions from India to Ireland, from Germany to Cajun country, mandated the immediate covering of all mirrors in the house when a loved one died. Mirrors were to be draped with crape, black mourning cloth, or simple bed linens.

The origins of the practice are mysterious and unclear. Oral history and folklore suggest multiple explanations. Perhaps the most common purpose in covering mirrors was to keep the deceased from seeing their reflection, lest they somehow be prevented from entering fully into the afterlife. The fear was that they'd be trapped in that thin seam between the living and the dead, belonging to neither world, eternally homeless. Since most people in the past died at home, all mirrors in the house were covered so that the loved one could be fully released unto death.

In a way, the death of a loved one positions *us* at a precipice. At this boundary line, we stand between what was and what will be. Often, it is excruciatingly difficult to accept this new reality. Maybe the act of covering the mirrors as a way of allowing the dead to proceed peacefully into the next life is less about *their* unwillingness to move on and more about *our* need to let them go. Perhaps we are the ones who are trapped in the in-between. We cower and wait and deny when, really, what we need is to proceed into a new life, a life without the person we love. We move into *our* own afterlife. It is life after the life of the one we love. We are never the same again.

• • • • •

I care a lot about what people think of me. Too much. Perception management is my favorite pastime. I'd much rather be the hero than the victim. I like people to think of me as someone with a good head on her shoulders, the person you can count on most when things are flying off the rails. Maybe it's just me, but I suspect most of us are born with this propensity to try to prove ourselves *to* ourselves and to one another. And maybe to God.

For me, it's an inclination that I'm certain was exacerbated by years of working with humanitarians. In my experience, it's fairly common for aid workers, social workers, emergency healthcare workers, and first responders—the folks who show up when all hell breaks loose—to make every effort to maintain a brave and stalwart exterior. The traditional way of proving your brass in the field of aid work is to appear tough and somewhat unaffected by suffering. Seasoned aid workers "push through." In their minds, vacations are for sissies, time off is for the entitled, and therapy is for the fragile. Only novices cry at the sight of a slum or a refugee camp. At least, that's how many of us think.

In her book *The Idealist's Survival Kit*, humanitarian psychologist Alessandra Pigni observes that aid workers have no problem sharing with incredible candidness personal stories recounting bad bouts of malaria or stomach amoebas. It's true. We'll divulge all the gory details of the time we lost our lunch on a UN flight, or the time we spent an entire week on the floor of a latrine in some far-flung corner of the world. But we will never talk about the refugee camp that wrecked us emotionally, the AIDS orphan who stole our heart, or the aerial bombardment that left us forever jumpy at the sound of fireworks. Pigni writes: "There's a form of heroic narrative that is somehow built into the non-profit work culture...Talking about personal suffering is taboo among many do-gooders. People would rather be infected with the plague than admit that they are mentally and emotionally shattered."[2]

Why is it so hard to admit that we *are* shattered? Why am I so embarrassed by my grief? After all, I'd spent my career trying to convince aid workers to be more vulnerable! Why, when my own world crumbled, did I become so hell-bent on maintaining my dignity, on not allowing bereavement to get the better of me? My natural predisposition to curate, to perform, to "toughen up," and to self-scrutinize went into overdrive. The temptation toward vanity may be especially strong when we are required to reckon with the humiliation of death. We "rage, rage against the dying of the light."[3] We refuse to admit what we all know to be true. Death *can* get the better of you, steals the very best of you, in fact.

But oh, did I rage.

In some traditional Jewish homes, the mirrors are still covered during *shivah*, the weeklong period of mourning after the death of a loved one. One reason for this is a conviction that those in mourning should be given the space to focus solely on their grief and their love for the person who died.[4] The mirror might interfere with that process, distracting the mourner with superficial concerns about appearance or vanity. A mourner might be tempted to check their hair or makeup, might become preoccupied with the dark circles under their eyes or the hollowness in their cheeks. They might begin to worry that others are judging them. They might begin to judge themselves.

Pride makes a terrible companion on the road of grief. Grief and trauma responses are not a performance. There is nothing to prove. Jen Pollock Michel writes, "We don't get good at grief. Suffering is inventive."[5] Bereavement is rarely a flattering look. No one ever becomes totally proficient in sorrow. It makes fools of us all, can make us feel like we are going crazy. Death, King Solomon tells us, is unyielding (see Song of Songs 8:6). Grief just doesn't quit. It's unrelenting.

The writings of Jewish mystics underscore the belief that staring obsessively at one's reflection can lead to arrogance. They teach that the act of gazing in the mirror can give power to evil spirits, which are particularly prevalent during seasons of death and mourning. It was thought that spirits might even attach themselves to a reflection if a mourner peered at themselves for too long.[6] This is another possible explanation for why mirrors were covered in a shivah home. Self-scrutiny leaves us especially vulnerable to attack by the spiritual forces of darkness.

I know well the "demonization" brought on by grief. The feeling that you've been exposed or violated. The loss of control. The wounding, the exploitation.

The feeling that you are going mad.

• • • • •

Celtic mythology tells the story of a beautiful young woman named Mis, who had raven black hair, deep dark eyes, and pale porcelain skin. Her father was the powerful ruler Daire Doidgheal, who set out from his homeland in Europe to invade Ireland and fight the famed warrior Fionn mac Cumhaill. The fierce battle lasted a year and a day on the western coast of County Kerry, Ireland. Fionn eventually defeated Daire and his warriors. In the aftermath of the bloodbath, Mis, who had traveled to Ireland with her father, frantically searched through the dead and dying bodies on the beach, desperate to find her beloved father.

At last, she found his decapitated body. Overcome by her grief, she flung herself on his corpse and began licking his wounds as if she were an injured animal. When she realized he was gone from her forever, her spirit broke and her mind slipped into a world of madness. She howled and screamed, rising up into the air like a crazed bird. She flew away from the beach and into a desolate mountain range in western Ireland that would someday take her name.

There, among the vales and peaks of Sliabh Mis, she lived as a wild creature, growing fur and feathers and long sharp claws. She would tear apart any animal or human she met and could run as fast as the wind. She had shape-shifted from a beautiful young woman to an untamed beast. Grief was the conduit for her grim transformation. She was so feared by the people of County Kerry that they dared not go near the forbidden mountains of Mis.[7]

Mythologist and folklorist Sharon Blackie writes:

> Sometimes madness seems like the only possible response to the insanity of the civilised world; sometimes, holding ourselves together is not an option, and the only way forward is to allow ourselves to fall apart. As the story of Mis shows, that madness can represent an extreme form of initiation, a trigger for profound transformation…This old story shows us a brutal descent into darkness during which all illusions are stripped away and old belief systems evaporate, and in doing so it suggests that the extremities of

madness or mental breakdown, with their prolonged, out-of-control descent into the unknown, might offer us a path through which we can come to terms with the truth.[8]

Here's the truth: Grief changes you. Even if you don't descend into full-on madness as Mis did, life after deep loss can *feel* like madness. The day after my sister died, I awoke from a fevered sleep, took a shower, and combed my hair. Suddenly, I couldn't remember which side of my head I parted my hair on. I'd been parting my hair on the same side of my head since the mid-'90s. *I must be going crazy*, I thought. I peered into the mirror, and I hardly recognized myself. It was as if I'd aged twenty years in three weeks. I'd lost nearly fifteen pounds and any confidence I'd ever had that I could remotely predict the future.

For months, I felt like a zombie. There was a constant ringing in my ears and time seemed like it had come to a grinding halt. I couldn't keep track of anything. I was constantly losing my keys, my purse, my phone. For months, I would forget what I was saying midsentence. I would get mixed up in meetings at work and stumble ineptly through presentations. My email in-box would pile up. I would begin typing responses but then be unable to decide what to say. And then, when friends or colleagues would show concern or ask me if I was okay, I would feel insulted and embarrassed that the facade of fortitude wasn't holding up like I thought it was.

Grief can upend domestic status and wreck family structures. Spouses become widows, daughters become orphans, siblings become the only child, as I did. I didn't know how to live *without* a sister. Our family of origin had been reduced by 25 percent. How do you pick up the pieces of a shattered family structure at a time when you have no energy to rebuild anything?

I would get angry at people, snap about things that never used to bother me. Minor inconveniences, like a clogged drain or a bill that needed paying, would send me spiraling. I had almost no capacity for stress and my feelings were easily hurt. Any character flaw or personal struggle I'd had to begin with was exacerbated.

It wasn't just my behavior that changed. My worldview began to shift. Truths I once held dear no longer seemed reliable. My theology felt shaky. Faith narratives began to give way under the weight of so much bewilderment. In many ways, when it came to my beliefs about God and myself and the world, I felt like I was starting again from scratch. Minuscule doubts became colossal; tiny uncertainties transformed into monsters.

Grief is like water. It follows gravity. It finds the lowest part of you and hollows it out even more. It exploits your weaknesses. Grief goes where it wants with or without an invitation. It seeps into the empty spaces. It cannot be harnessed or redirected, at least not easily. It branches out from the headwaters of the main event into hundreds of tributaries. Few areas of your life remain untouched. New losses are discovered almost daily. Life progresses without the one you love in it, and you miss them all over again with every new season and every turn in the road.

So how does the story of Mis end? A gentle young harpist named Dubh Ruis went searching for her in the woods on the mountainside. He built her a shelter of branches and moss. He played his harp for her and offered her bread. He took her to a pool of clear water, not to show Mis her hideous reflection, but to wash her clean. He kissed her and held her until eventually, over time, she transformed back into a lovely woman again, not the same as before but beautiful in a new way. The young harpist guarded Mis's humanity. He called it forth. He was present and patient despite the savage nature of Mis's grief. Mis was remade by love. She was loved back to life. Yes, death is unyielding. But, as the bridegroom Solomon writes, so is love.

• • • • •

Most scholars agree that the first book of the Bible ever written was Job. It is compelling to me that when God set out to reveal Himself to humanity through the written word, the first topic He wanted to address was the problem of pain. There is a tenderness in that choice, an acknowledgment that the universal human experience is suffering. Grief is an ancient sentiment, as old as time and as ubiquitous as breath. Whether you are wealthy or poor, godly or godless, foolish or wise, you will know the kneading pain of loss, catastrophe, or illness at some point in your life.

Job is the personification of bereavement. His wealth and possessions are lost to marauders and firestorms. His children all die in a windstorm. His health is overtaken by an excruciating disease. Satan has it out for him. In the story's telling, the veil that divides the physical and the spiritual realms is lifted, and we are given a behind-the-scenes view of the battle that rages around us, the struggle that "is not against flesh and blood, but against the rulers, against the authorities, against the powers of this dark world and against the spiritual forces of evil in the heavenly realms" (Eph. 6:12).

As the story unfolds, we find that Job is not alone in his grief. In two short verses in chapter 2, we meet his wife. She speaks briefly in a manner that seems mocking of Job: "Are you still maintaining your integrity? Curse God and die!" (Job 2:9).

These are infamous lines, well known by a church that is wary of the wanton words of women. John Calvin referred to Job's wife as "Satan's tool," and Augustine called her "the devil's assistant."[9] I've tended to agree with those assessments. I've always dismissed Job's wife as unregenerate, unfaithful, weak, and fickle. I've scoffed at her inability to rise to the occasion.

That is, until I experienced grief.

Put yourself in the place of Job's wife for a moment. The life she had built shoulder to shoulder with her husband was lost. Their financial security was wiped out. Her children, all ten of them, were lost in one day. The bodies she had birthed into the world, the mouths that had nursed at her breasts, the souls she had loved and nurtured were crushed all at once in a moment of natural violence. If children are the heartbeat of a mother, it's a wonder that her heart didn't stop that day. I imagine the disbelief, the unbearable agony. I imagine how desirable death must have seemed to her in that moment. We cannot talk about the suffering of Job without acknowledging the suffering of his wife. She must have been driven nearly mad with mourning.

We meet this woman even as her husband, Job, is walking through the rituals of grief. He has shaved his head and torn his garments. He has worshipped. When his wife approaches, Job is sitting in the ashes, scraping his wounds with a piece of broken pottery. It is from this place of ancient ritual that Job hears his wife's outburst, and then inserts a word of grace into her life: "You speak as one of the foolish women would speak" (Job 2:10 ESV). Theologian Christopher Ash notes, "In kindness he does not actually call her a foolish woman. But he says that what she has suggested is not worthy of her. She has spoken under stress, as if she were a fool."[10] Job must know his wife to be wise and certainly not a fool. But grief has changed her.

Then, from this realm of ritual, Job asks a simple question that invites his wife into a space of wisdom and acceptance: "Shall we accept good from God, and not trouble?" (Job 2:10).

I cannot excuse the words of Job's wife. Nor do I condemn her. I know the foolish and hateful thoughts that arise from a place of maddening grief. I remember feeling resentful of recovering COVID-19 patients who came off ventilators, because my sister had never come off her ventilator. I remember cursing the Duchess of Cambridge, who announced she was pregnant with her *third* child, even as I mourned the loss of my first. The day after I arrived home from Iraq, I threw a broom at Tim's head because he had not swept the living room floor to my standards (apparently, my standards of cleanliness become significantly higher than normal in the immediate aftermath of trauma).

There are angry thoughts, vindictive thoughts, thoughts that are beyond comprehension under the normal circumstances of your life. I remember thinking at one point, as Job's wife did, *Maybe I should just give up*. That thought was not worthy of me. And yet, there it was: Death seemed to be suspended before me as a merciful option. The invitation was strong; at times, even stronger than the invitation to live.

Most of us probably feel like we don't have the luxury of succumbing to a complete and total breakdown. There's no time for it! Bills need to be paid and babies need to be cared for. People depend on us. That's a heavy burden, but also, perhaps, a grace. It keeps us tethered to the world.

Wendell Berry writes this in his book *Hannah Coulter* about a young woman whose life is marked by grief: "The living can't quit living because the world has turned terrible and people they love and need are killed. They can't because they don't. The light that shines in darkness and never goes out calls them on into life…It calls them into work and pleasure, goodness and beauty, and the company of other loved ones."[11] Life, with all its demands, responsibilities, and yes, joys, insists that we press on.

It used to seem strange to me that family members of the deceased are listed in the obituary as "survivors." The term seems to imply that you were struck by the same malady as the one who died, only you pulled through it somehow while they succumbed. My grandmother struggled with pneumonia in her final days, and my sister battled the flu and static seizures. I didn't experience either of these illnesses at the time, and yet I am referred to as a survivor. The term "survivor" denotes withstanding some kind of disaster, a shipwreck or a car crash or a terrorist attack. It indicates a near miss, a brush with death, or a close call of some kind. It seems to say that death had plans for you, but those plans were thwarted through some divine intervention or miracle of human strength.

I understand the term a little better now. Grief is, in many ways, a fight for survival. You do battle with death, wage war against hopelessness. Instead of quitting, you get up and put one foot in front of the other. You go to counseling. You pray. You cry on the shoulders of friends and take a walk. You watch reruns of *Seinfeld* and change your kid's diaper. Perhaps most importantly, you give yourself grace. You endure. Survival is the only real option.

There are some even darker and more foreboding legends that account for the tradition of covering mirrors after death. Some Jewish historians attribute the practice to the belief that the angel of death had visited the household, and that if a mourner saw the reflection of this grim reaper, they, too, would perish.[12] This is not the only tradition that cites danger in the mirror for loved ones left behind. Many cultures maintain the belief that if a relative or friend sees their own image in a mirror while grieving, they will be the next to experience severe illness or even death.[13]

As it turns out, some people cover the mirrors in order to survive.

• • • • •

There are some catastrophes in life that create a *before* and an *after*. We all know the moment, the thing that changed us so irrevocably that it feels like we have led two lives. The life before seems to have existed in an alternate universe. The one after is perilous and unknown, but it is here to stay. We find ourselves in the aftermath of an atom bomb explosion, desperately searching for the "silver lining to the mushroom cloud," as my brother-in-law, Dan, likes to say.

I'm not sure we ever find it.

Grief changes us. It was not a change I invited into my life. It was not a change I was ready for. Nevertheless, there it is. I am not the same.

I didn't like my new self at first. People ask me sometimes if I sense my sister's presence still, if I am haunted by her ghost. I am not. But I am often haunted by the old me, the ghost of my former self, my former life. I miss the me who didn't know what it was to lose something I loved so much, who didn't know in her bones how fragile and frightening life can be. I liked that Amanda. She was nice. She was sharp and witty. She was responsible and usually on time to things. She was fun.

Perhaps our ancestors' fears of looking in the mirror after a personal loss were not unfounded. When a loved one dies, you die a little too. But this death to self, at least in the spiritual sense, is a familiar motif for those of us who read the Bible. We should not fear it or resist it. In fact, this is precisely the paradox that grief introduces. We must fight to reject the invitation of death, must insist on our own survival. And yet we must *also* embrace the idea that we are no longer who we once were, that our old selves *have* died. We are new.

The *death to self* to which all followers of Christ are called, whether blessed or bereft, is a death to self-reliance and to egotism. It is a death to religious performance and pious achievement. It is a letting go of our expectations and of our tightly held personal agendas. It is a release of our careful curation but also an embrace, instead, of authenticity.

Somehow, someway, God makes room for new life. Little by little, God remakes us. This process of resurrection is most hindered by our pride, our self-righteous resistance. We have to be willing to accept the untidiness of it all, to succumb to its slowness, its disruption, its lack of quick conclusions. Like Mis, who was loved back to life with time, intentionality, and the tenderness of the one who cared for her the most, we can find a new way of being in the world. We can be remade by love.

"It has to get messy before it gets clean!" This is a mantra my mother would repeat with cheery conviction every time we undertook the process of spring-cleaning at our house. She'd strip the beds and empty the bookshelves, pull out all the broken toys and half-eaten graham crackers from beneath the furniture. Brooms, mops, vacuum cleaners, and dust rags littered the floor. Life was upended until it was put back together, sparkling, orderly, and brand-new. It had to get messy before it got clean. As my sister once wrote, my mom's mantra is "a philosophy that pretty much sums up every meaningful experience of my life."[14] For me, this includes grief. You must accept that the house is being turned upside down. It has to get messy before it gets clean.

You may not like who you are for a while, maybe a long while, after grief. It is wise, I think, to cover your mirrors after the death of someone or something you love. Suspend your expectations of yourself. Stop the performance. Stop worrying about appearances. Live fully into the new normal. Ask your friends to cover the mirrors for you. Accept grace from others, and show grace to yourself.

I do not think we can say of grief, "This, too, shall pass." There is no going back. A new landscape has been carved by grief's rushing water, and if we are to survive, we must make a home in it, however that might look. For a time, it may feel like a wilderness. But there is an invitation to wisdom and acceptance in this wasteland. There is a new you to discover, and it may be a holy encounter. And in fact, the wilderness is a great place for death and rebirth, for getting lost and then being found.

And sometimes, like our ancestors' experience of glimpsing their reflection in a mirror for the first time, the encounter may be transcendent.

CHAPTER 3

TELLING THE BEES

(FEAR)

*What is your life? You are a mist that appears
for a little while and then vanishes.*
—James 4:14

When Tim first told me he wanted to start keeping bees, I was skeptical. I imagined swarms of angry bees chasing me across the yard, the toxins from dozens of angry stings nearly asphyxiating me and sending me to the hospital. Bees seemed risky to me, and I was afraid. Besides, how much honey could a single hive produce, anyway? Would it really be worth all the learning and labor required to become an apiarist?

Tim is always the more optimistic of the two of us. Where I

saw danger and drudgery, he saw the potential of mason jars filled with golden honey, beeswax candles, and a well-pollinated garden. I eventually gave in and supported him, but I refused to ever go near the bee box. Five years later, we now have two thriving hives, situated up behind the house, to the left of the vegetable patch. We love our bees. But I still keep my distance.

I'm glad that in the end, I eventually did support my husband's apicultural endeavor. As I type this, I'm staring at a five-gallon bucket full of decadent honey. It's harvest season right now and Tim has been busy with the hives, removing frames of honeycomb, scraping the wax cappings off the cells, and spinning the honey out into the extractor. Truth be told, you can make a pretty good profit off a strong hive; we've got jars lined up in the hallway ready to be sold to our friends and neighbors and more than enough to enjoy ourselves.

There was once a superstition in old Europe that said bees will not thrive if they belong to a quarrelsome household. Apparently, bees don't like contentious masters and, legend has it, they hate swearing.[1] My marriage has not been perfect by a long shot, but it's been happy, one of those slow-burn love affairs, a fondness that has mileage to it and a partnership where little is left unsaid or unknown. Our friendship has aged well, and I am grateful for it. We are content and the bees seem content too.

I recently asked Tim about this curious superstition, and it turns out there could be some truth behind the folklore. Bees are incredibly talented at picking up on emotions. Mammals release chemical pheromones when they feel threatened or agitated. If an upset human enters the space around the hive, the bees will "smell" it and might start acting funny. Moreover, if a beekeeper's movements are too hurried or frantic, bees might become aggressive in an attempt to defend the hive. This is why laid-back folks tend to make the best apiarists. They know how to calm themselves before approaching the hive. They work smoothly, at a measured and relaxed pace. Like Tim.

Recently, he and I sat up late on our front porch talking about the bees. Even though it was still summertime, the mountain air always turned a bit brisk in the evenings. We shivered in the heavy, humid chill, and the darkness was noisy with crickets and katydids. We breathed in the scent of the season's last blooms and watched the clouds drift past the nearly full moon. We could hear the horses down in the valley crossing the creek, headed to the barn for the night, so we knew it would soon be time for us to sleep as well. Inspired by all the bee talk, I told Tim maybe I should consider getting a bee suit and trying my hand at managing a hive.

"Oh, it would be a disaster if you went up to the hives," he said, and laughed, half joking, half serious. When I asked him why, he explained to me how sensitive bees are to fear. They smell it. And no doubt, they would smell it on me.

• • • • •

C. S. Lewis, in his renowned opus on suffering *A Grief Observed*, wrote: "No one ever told me grief felt so much like fear."[2] This fear is often born out of that terrible education that loss bestows on the bereaved. What you knew intellectually becomes true experientially: Death is real. Life as you know it can end.

Existence is fragile. On the one hand, the human body is remarkably resilient, able to survive cancers, violent car wrecks, and devastating wounds of war. On the other hand, the human body is made of supple flesh and brittle bone. Vital organs beat, inflate, process, and pump, all behind a meager protective barrier of rib, muscle, and skin. A tiny piece of shrapnel that strikes just the wrong spot can end a life in a moment. A split second of carelessness at the wheel can result in a deadly car crash. A microscopic virus can spread like wildfire, invade bodies, shut down the world, and leave us bereft of millions of loved ones.

Our seemingly secure and affluent lives may have led us to forget that anyone who lives in a body is painfully exposed. We fancy ourselves as invincible. These days life expectancy has soared to 78.7 years,[3] and medical advancements render most diseases, disorders, or accidents treatable. In our minds, death has become an avoidable outcome, a consequence of medical mismanagement. Historian Philippe Aries writes, "Death has ceased to be accepted as a natural, necessary phenomenon. Death is a failure, a 'business lost.' This is an attitude of the doctor, who claims the control of death as his mission in life. But the doctor is merely a spokesperson for society."[4]

Seven hundred years ago, an entire continent was reminded with jarring severity that death was anything but controllable. The Black Plague of the late 1340s is believed to have wiped out one-third of the population of Europe and parts of Asia. Mortality lurked around every corner and the stench of death filled the air as bodies piled up in the streets. Many historians believe that it was during the plague years that the West first began to abandon many of its grief traditions, as there were simply too many bodies to ritualistically mourn.[5] Moreover, 40 percent of parish clergy, the men who would traditionally perform the rites of death, succumbed to the disease themselves.[6]

Understandably, the cryptic and abrupt nature of death was a cultural obsession during this time. Before there were microscopes or germ theory or diagnostic capabilities, illness was terribly mysterious. There was no reasonable explanation for why this particular outbreak was so catastrophic. The ominous presence of death was palpable and deeply ingrained in society's consciousness. Fear stalked the streets.

Perhaps as a way of processing this fear, the artistic genre of *danse macabre*, or the dance of death, became very popular in the years following the Black Plague. In these paintings and frescoes, gleeful skeletons or mummies dance and play instruments, and then invite the living from all walks of life—kings, peasants, merchants, and clergy—to join them. The moral purpose of *danse macabre* is to remind people that the hour of death is uncertain but inevitable for all, no matter your station in life.[7]

Philippe Aries writes, "Society refuses to participate in the emotion of the bereaved. This is a way of denying the presence of death in practice, even if one accepts its reality in principle."[8] It shouldn't take a global pandemic to remind us that death is real and life is precarious, but it certainly does serve as a wake-up call. Everything we've worked for can be gone in a moment. Plans are derailed. Fortunes are lost. Health fails and hearts break. All this fragility begs the question: Who even are we if death can so effectively and instantaneously stop us in our tracks?

I know the experience of running a million miles an hour in my hurried, happy, and secure life: work, a possible promotion, babies and playdates, church activities, a social life, house projects. And then, suddenly, everything comes to a crashing halt with one phone call.

This precarity that grief introduces casts a long shadow. For a while after a sudden loss, nothing feels good, and nothing feels safe. Innocuous situations can suddenly feel like an existential threat.

The simple medical procedure is an opportunity for calamity, the long-awaited vacation is a plane crash in the making, a relaxing family picnic is the inevitable calm before the storm. It's all a bit like some grim Rorschach inkblot test. Where others see happiness, I see a disaster waiting to happen.

These days, I can't even hold my daughter without wincing at the delicate nature of her existence. Her skin and bones in my arms feel so much like those of the children I held in Iraq. I know with too much specificity what kind of wounding would take her away from me. And the reality is that if I don't lose her, then she will lose me. I will die. Either way, this ends in grief. Sometimes the thought of it is just too much to bear.

• • • • •

Stay at home, pretty bees, fly not hence!
Mistress Mary is dead and gone! [9]

So ends the John Greenleaf Whittier poem "Telling the Bees," written in 1858. In the poem, Whittier tells the story of a man returning to the home of his lover after a season of absence, only to find the servant girl dolefully informing the bees that the woman he loves has died. The hives have all been draped in black cloth.

It is unclear exactly when the tradition of telling the bees emerged in Europe, but folklore surrounding bees is as old as civilization. In the ancient world, bees played a huge role in the mythological imagination and featured prominently in creation narratives from the Kalahari Desert region in Africa to Rome and to Egypt. [10] Our ancestors saw honeybees as a bridge between the natural world and the supernatural, between the land of the living and the land of the dead. Archaeologists have found images of bees etched on Bronze Age tombs,[11] and the renowned kings of Egypt were buried with honey.

Though the origin of the superstition of telling the bees is unknown, it may have emerged from the ancient Celtic belief that the soul of the dead would leave the body in the form of a bee. The ritual requires that you inform the family beehives when a member of the household, particularly the beemaster, has died, or else the bees will get sick, die, or fly away. This ritual seems to have been most prominent in the eighteenth and nineteenth centuries in Western Europe and the United States, and it has all but completely died out now.[12]

There was a proper way to "put bees in mourning," but the protocols varied from place to place. Hives were often covered in black crape, and some regional beliefs stipulated that you tap on each hive, one by one, with a house key before sharing the news.[13]

Some traditions required that you shout the news to the bees; others insisted that you whisper or sing the news. Some even specified that the words be scripted or rhyming. A verse heard sung in New Hampshire went like this: "Bees, bees, awake! / Your master is dead, / And another you must take."[14] A song heard in Oxfordshire, England, in the 1880s declared: "Bees, bees, your master's dead, an' now you must work for your missis."[15] In Buckinghamshire, people would tap on the hives three times and say, "Little Brownies, your master is dead." If the bees began to hum, it meant they had consented to remain in the hive.[16] Bees were also customarily invited to the funeral, and drink or food that had been provided at the service, such as wine or biscuits, was to be placed in front of the hive.[17]

While tradition held that bees were to be informed of all kinds of important family events such as weddings and births, communication about death seemed to be the most consequential. There are plenty of anecdotal stories of bees dying or leaving the hive because they had not been told of their master's death. An even older custom was to move the hives when a household member had passed, sometimes to the right and in other cases turned to face the door of the family home. This practice, known as ricking, was to signify that a profound change had occurred in the lives of the family members, and, in turn, in the lives of the bees.[18]

I wonder how this ritual of telling the bees played out for a family in mourning. How does one share the passing of a loved one while maintaining the relaxed serenity with which you are supposed to approach a hive of wary bees? How was a widow or servant or orphan supposed to reassure the bees when their own life had been turned upside down? No doubt, the ritual itself required that one momentarily collect oneself and calm the quickened spirit. The song was gentle, but the reality was cruel. And I wonder if the bees could smell the sadness underneath the composure. Could they smell the fear?

• • • • •

People talk about how in the aftermath of a tornado or a hurricane, they get lost in their own neighborhoods. The GPS points are the same but all the landmarks are gone. I get it. After my sister died, I felt lost in my own life.

The people we love most in the world serve as footholds in our lives. They are the bedrock, the infrastructure that stabilizes our meaning, our purpose, our schedules, and our activities. They bind together our past, present, and future. Each plays a specific role, relationally and practically, that no one else on earth ever can fill. This means that we all experience death and grief differently, depending on who died and when and how. Poet, artist, and minister Jan Richardson, who lost her husband suddenly after only four years of marriage, writes:

> Grief is piercingly particular…[It] shapes itself precisely to the details of our lives. It fits itself to our habits and routines, our relationships, our priorities, what we have organized our lives around—all that makes us who we are in this world. Because of this, no one will know our grief as we do. No one will inhabit it in the same way we do. No one will entirely understand what it is like to live with our specific shattering.[19]

Everyone I've ever loved who died took with them to the grave a function in my life that is irreplaceable. They were a link in the chain, a star in the constellation that made up my relational life. The people we love and lose share our everyday burdens: paying the bills, bringing home a paycheck, emptying the trash, changing diapers, or planning holiday gatherings. Life is a shared labor. There's nothing like losing a co-laborer to make you feel helpless and vulnerable.

Tim talks often about the important role each bee plays in the hive, how their rigid commitment to their assigned task is essential for the life and well-being of the colony. There are house bees who tend to the hive and intrepid field bees who scout and gather. There are guard bees and bees who work in the nursery. Then there are, of course, drones. These are the male bees whose only job is to mate with the queen and die immediately thereafter.

"It's a civilization, really," Tim tells me. "There's choreography, smoothness, and fluidity to the work. No one's running into each other." He laughs. Perhaps this is why the honeybee has become universally emblematic of industry and civic cooperation. Everyone from the monastics to the Freemasons to the Mormons has used the image of the beehive to symbolize the values of order, community, and shared labor.[20]

No role is as important as the queen's, whose responsibility as procreator ensures the continuation of the community. She is the lifeblood of the hive. "As the queen goes, so goes the hive," Tim tells me. If the queen is weak, the hive will be weak. If the queen dies, the hive will cease to exist. The bees are lost without her.

It's something Tim is always mindful of, always checking on. He knows that no matter the quality of his work and attention or the dedication of the scouts or foragers, there will be little to no honey if the queen isn't thriving. The relational, functional choreography is disrupted. It's the fear you live with as a beekeeper: the catastrophic loss of the one you most depend on.

• • • • •

Preachers and motivational speakers like to remind us that the command "Fear not" is the most common admonition in Scripture. I used to think that was a pretty cool sentiment.

Not anymore.

The truth is that I am *often* afraid. Very afraid. And I worry that to "fear not" is to be irresponsible, naive to the dangerous realities all around us. Fearlessness in the face of so much fragility seems arrogant and foolhardy. I've sworn to myself that I'll never be caught off guard again.

I'm not alone. Scripture is replete with the people of God bemoaning the brevity and unpredictability of life. Job laments that mortals "spring up like flowers and wither away; like fleeting shadows, they do not endure" (Job 14:2). After a debilitating illness, Hezekiah says, "Like a shepherd's tent my house has been pulled down and taken from me. Like a weaver I have rolled up my life, and he has cut me off from the loom; day and night you made an end of me" (Isa. 38:12). David sings that "everyone is but a breath, even those who seem secure. Surely everyone goes around like a mere phantom" (Ps. 39:5–6).

Nevertheless, we *are* called to courage. But how? How do we go to work knowing our labors could be lost? How do we invest in a calling that could fall by the wayside? How do we confront evil when we know that sometimes it wins?

And how do we love when love can be lost? How do we remain tender toward one another, through a plague, through pestilence? How did a mother give her uninhibited love to her toddler in the 1800s, when childhood mortality rates soared to 46 percent?[21] How do you form friendships when there are cancers and car wrecks? How do you devote your life to aid work when there will always be terrorists, there will always be earthquakes, there will always be famines? How do you take the risk of love without being filled with fear?

Perhaps courage is not the same as self-assuredness. We can sometimes conflate bravery with bluster, heroism with hubris. James warns about this kind of pretentious confidence:

> Now listen, you who say, "Today or tomorrow we will go
> to this or that city, spend a year there, carry on business
> and make money." Why, you do not even know what will

happen tomorrow. What is your life? You are a mist that appears for a little while and then vanishes. Instead, you ought to say, "If it is the Lord's will, we will live and do this or that." As it is, you boast in your arrogant schemes. All such boasting is evil. (James 4:13–16)

Inherent in this reproach is the truth that we are all limited, that the outcome is always unpredictable, and that we don't always have all the answers. These are true but tough pills to swallow. The solution, that there is someone—God—who is in control and knows all things, disrupts our self-importance. We are always drawn to the forbidden fruit. We want to possess all outcomes, all knowledge, all explanations. We want to be in the driver's seat. We are disinclined to trust anyone but ourselves. While God's sovereignty is the safest resting place, it chafes against our pride.

I went to Iraq in the wintertime. While I was gone, Tim had to check the hive to see how the bees were faring through the cold mountain weather. When he opened the lid, all he found were a few dozen dead bees lying in the bee box. The rest of the bees had apparently absconded. The word "abscond" literally means "to leave in secret." The bees had outwitted our attempts to master them. It all felt very clandestine. Tim had a few ideas on why the bees had flown away; maybe there were mites or maybe he had winterized the hive too early, but there's no way we'll ever know for sure. Whatever the reason, they had vanished.

Death doesn't always give a reason. Victims of the fourteenth-century plague had no idea where the black boils had come from. No doctor could fully explain my miscarriages to me. It is a mystery why my healthy thirty-seven-year-old sister started experiencing static seizures. But our modern, Western brains like to have an explanation for everything. When a global crisis happens, we all simultaneously turn to Twitter to provide our own geopolitical take, whether or not we are qualified to do so. We blame, we assign responsibility, we virtue-signal.

Arrogance is often the protest of the insecure. Beneath our bluster and braggadocio, we are all frightened children, clinging desperately to our security blankets but knowing full well they might be ripped away from us at any moment. We are spoiled and have become very used to the idea that if we want something, we should be able to have it. If I want an explanation, surely it's out there, and surely I am entitled to it.

Our inclination to explain away suffering is an indication of how reticent we are to simply lament as a society, to admit our weakness. When our understandings of cause and effect, control, and reciprocity are all disrupted, it's humbling. Bewilderment is an experience we aren't accustomed to in our culture. But this humiliation and bewilderment are at the heart of the death wail. They are the ingredients of grief. Death *is* humiliating. It's mortifying. It's incomprehensible. So many of the psalms of lament begin with the question "Why?" And there isn't always an answer.

We search longingly for answers to the tragedies great and small in our lives. The hope is that we'll be able to wrap our brains around the loss, assuage our fears, and perhaps avoid catastrophe next time. While Tim was eager to know why his hive had failed, I was desperate to know why the world was such an ugly place, why God would allow terrorist and militant groups to use toddlers as human shields.

"Sometimes, it just happens," my own toddler likes to earnestly say when she spills her milk or scrapes her knee. I usually try to piece together the events that led up to her accident and coach her on how to avoid such mishaps in the future. But maybe what she's asking of me is to just *be* with her, in her frustration, in her hurt.

It takes a lot of courage to simply be sad, to relinquish control and call off the search for an explanation. "If the Lord wills it…" The faith a statement like that requires is born of a supernatural bravery. It is not bravery that comes from control, confidence in my own strength, or certainty of outcome. It is a bravery that trusts in the Lord despite the mystery, one that invests itself fully into the labor no matter the precarity of the future. It is a bravery that trusts in the beauty of love, knowing at the core that it is worth the risk. It is a courage that is "all in" on the daily gamble life offers us. It is a courage that lives openhandedly, as James calls us to live. It is a courage that accepts. It is a bravery born of a holy humiliation.

Faith shines at its brightest when it is confronted with the darkness of fear. Or as Daniel Taylor writes in his book *The Myth of Certainty*, "Where there is doubt, faith has its reason for being… Doubt makes its claims, even daily, and they are respected, but they do not determine the character of my life."[22]

The rituals of acceptance, of calming oneself, of regrouping require this kind of bravery. I wonder if in telling the bees, our ancestors were really telling themselves something: Yes, everything has changed. Yes, life is precarious. But don't give up. All is not lost. Trust your caretakers. "Fly not hence."

• • • • •

Shortly after I found out I was pregnant with my second daughter, Lois, I was sitting in our living room reading a book in the sunshine that was coming through the windows. Those were the early days of the pandemic. Our normally busy schedule had come to a grinding halt under isolation and quarantine guidelines, so we passed the lazy, lonely summer days as a family reading, taking walks, and planting our garden. The anniversary of my sister's death had just passed and I was beginning to languish under the heavy weight of early pregnancy symptoms—nausea, exhaustion, dizziness. All my emotions simmered just beneath the surface of my skin. After three miscarriages, I wondered if this tired, grieving body of mine could sustain a life that was as small as a poppy seed and delicate as a dream. I was anxious. I was happy. I was afraid.

As I dozed with my book on my chest that afternoon, I was awakened by a faint and unusual sound through the screen door, a low humming that seemed to be coming from behind the house, but then suddenly from the side and then in front of the house. I stepped out onto the porch. It was a bright day with hardly a cloud in the sky, but suddenly the landscape took on a gray hue and the sun seemed vaguely obscured.

Tim rounded the corner of the house with a puzzled look on his face. Then it dawned on him. "I think the bees are swarming," he said with his usual sense of calm. I immediately panicked. What did it mean for the bees to swarm? Would we lose all of them? What would happen to the honey? Should I close all the windows? Would the bees try to attack us?

Tim reminded me of the importance of staying calm and told me to just watch. There we stood, as literally thousands upon thousands of bees flew in an undulating circular pattern all around us. The buzzing sound grew louder and louder, until it was almost deafening. The sky darkened and we held our breath.

Tim told me later that a swarm is a loss, but not as devastating as one would think. Bees typically swarm because the hive is overcrowded or because they sense their queen is growing old and weak. Half of the colony stays in the old hive with a new queen, and the rest swarm with the old queen to find a new spot to call home, where they will presumably begin raising up a new queen as well. Swarming is natural, Tim says. He regrets that he didn't have another hive ready, that he lost the swarm. But he compares a swarm to a wildfire. It's a startling experience to be sure, but it allows for old things to die and makes space for new things to grow.

Eventually, the buzzing died down and the skies began to clear. Tim began walking around our property, his neck craned, peering up at the tops of the trees. Eventually he pointed to a high branch in an old pine tree. "I think they've picked a place to congregate," he said. He told me that scout bees would go out later and look for a permanent home for the new colony.

If you've ever experienced bees swarming, you know what a surreal experience it is. You feel swept up in some frightful phenomenon that you have no control over, a natural ritual that is as old as the earth, orderly but chaotic, eerie but awe-inspiring. With no warning, the bees made a dramatic departure, and enveloped our home in their communal drone before finally subsiding into their typical, tranquil existence. There was no way of knowing why they had picked that particular day of all days. Nevertheless, there we were, caught up in the din and disquiet of it all.

I guess a great many things had happened that we'd neglected to tell them.

CHAPTER 4

SITTING SHIVAH

(PRESENCE)

As the deer pants for streams of water,
so my soul pants for you, my God.
My soul thirsts for God, for the living God.
When can I go and meet with God?
My tears have been my food day and night.

—Psalm 42:1–3

Here's the problem with having had a really easy time of it growing up: when you do finally experience tragedy, as we all inevitably do, you are totally unprepared for it.

I'd been raised in a loving home by two generous and compassionate parents. I'd had a big sister who looked out for me and a community of friends who supported me. We'd never been rich, but there was always food on the table and a roof over our heads. I'd been fortunate enough to pursue higher education. I'd had an amazing experience living abroad in India after college and found a job I loved as a nonprofit worker shortly after my arrival home. I'd married a kind man who worked hard, laughed easily, and never kept a record of any wrong I'd committed against him. I was good at my religion, admired for my character, and well situated in my social surroundings. I was healthy, privileged, and secure. I was in control of my life.

Kate Bowler is one of the world's premier scholars of the theology and practice of the prosperity gospel movement in America. Bowler was diagnosed with stage four cancer at the age of thirty-five. As she processed both her experience of studying the health and wealth gospel and her own personal encounter with suffering and mortality, she wrote:

> I would love to report that what I found in the prosperity gospel was something so foreign and terrible to me that I was warned away, but what I discovered was both familiar and painfully sweet: the promise that I could curate my life, minimize my losses, and stand on my successes. And no matter how many times I rolled my eyes at the creed's outrageous certainties, I craved them just the same. I had my own Prosperity Gospel, a flowering weed grown in with all the rest.[1]

When Tim and I began to struggle with infertility, I assumed it was a blip on the radar. My well-ordered, finely tuned life must have simply short-circuited for a moment. Surely it wouldn't be long before things got back on track and life went back to normal.

Back to good. God was testing us. Or teaching us. No doubt, we would patiently and righteously endure, and He would reward us with a baby in time. Our good choices and positive thinking combined with God's good graces would right the ship. God may not be in the business of prosperity, but He is in the business of happiness, right?

Sure enough, I found out I was pregnant after a couple of years of struggling and a few doctors' consultations. Back on track. Back to good.

And then, the baby died.

That may have been the moment when I realized that just because your life has been easy up to a point doesn't mean it will continue in the same manner. It was then that I realized that the gospel may not always result in the emotional and experiential prosperity I had come to expect, and that God didn't always behave in the way I thought He should. God had disappointed me—not in the rainy Saturday or middle school breakup kind of way. He had disappointed me in the soul-crushing, life-altering kind of way.

Even then, I had no idea what was coming, that there were more miscarriages in the future and that I was going to lose my only sister. In many ways, I'd been a bystander to tragedy for many years, having lived in an Indian orphanage after college and then serving as a nonprofit worker and international disaster responder later. I'd always felt like I lived in the suburbs of other people's trauma, so I fancied myself cognizant and well prepared for loss. When I found myself at the epicenter of my own tragedy, I realized I was completely inept.

The language of the American evangelical church had informed many of my assumptions about suffering. Church people have a way of approaching hardship with an air of pretense and a load of half-truths that don't get you very far when you are in the throes of bereavement: Everything happens for a reason, right? God won't give you more than you can handle, right? Just pray, and that peace that passes all understanding will wash over your body from head to toe, right? The presence of God will descend upon you like a dove from heaven, right?

The problem was, *that peace* and *that presence* sure didn't feel like I thought it would.

I had assumed up until recently that peace was primarily a feeling, and a pleasant one at that—comforting, gratifying, reassuring. I had also assumed that the feeling of God's presence would be much the same. In my mind, God's presence was supposed to be, if anything, affable. I'm now learning, thanks to the work and writings of folks like Lisa Sharon Harper, that the biblical understanding of peace (*shalom*) has less to do with feelings and more to do with a state of being. It's about rightness, correct action within relationships, and wholeness.[2] Ease does not always equal wholeness. Comfort is not always rightness. In fact, in the Bible, God's presence is very often associated with fire and judgment. Job was terrified by it (see Job 13:21; 23:15). Isaiah said it induces the same kind of pain as is experienced by a woman in labor (see Isa. 26:17). God's presence is ferocious at times, an anointing of flame. Does His presence bring refinement? Yes. Happiness and tranquility? Not always.

When my sister died, and God didn't show up in the way I thought He would, I was completely lost. I longed for that still, small, comforting voice, not the whirlwind of fire I was experiencing. Never have I felt more betrayed by God than in that moment, not because she died, but because He didn't seem to have any interest in alleviating the sheer discomfort of my emotions. It was like I had lost my sister *and* God all at once.

• • • • •

Judaism has a rich abundance of grief rituals that have remained largely intact over the centuries. It designates and names the different periods of grief after a loss. During the twenty-four to forty-eight hours between the actual death and the funeral, the relative of the deceased is said to be in a state of *aninut*. This is the most intense and disorienting stage of grief, as the shock of the loss is absorbed and necessary funeral arrangements are made. *Shivah,* which literally means "seven," is the seven-day period of mourning following the funeral. During shivah, the needs of the mourners are met by visiting family and friends. Mourners stay home and are not expected to work or attend any outside functions.

Sheloshim is the thirty-day period after the funeral when the mourner slowly begins to integrate back into the normal rhythms and routines of life, but still refrains from attending public celebrations or participating in any form of entertainment. The end of *sheloshim* concludes the official period of mourning and is often marked by a special prayer or memorial service. For mourners grieving the loss of a parent, the formal time of mourning is extended another eleven months. The first year of mourning is known as the *shnat ha-evel.*

Finally, *yahrzeit* is the yearly anniversary of the loved one's death. It is observed annually by lighting a *yahrzeit* candle, which burns for twenty-four hours in memory of the loved one who died.[3]

Traditional Jewish grieving rituals require a strict immersion into pain. Mourners sit on low stools or crates to signify that they have been brought low in grief—hence the term "sitting shivah." In Orthodox tradition, mourners are to refrain from wearing fresh clothing, playing or listening to music, reading entertaining books or watching television, or engaging in physical intimacy with a spouse. They are even expected to refrain from warm baths or showers, which are seen to be physically comforting. A mourner should not greet people in the usual way (as in "Hello" or "Shalom"). Rather, they are to simply nod their heads in solemn acknowledgment of a visitor. Food can be delivered by friends, but it is expected to be simple and nourishing, no fancy desserts or indulgent sweets.[4] It's as if no pleasure the world has to offer should distract or detract from the experience of sorrow.

Our mainstream, modern-day American culture avoids pain whenever possible. We have been conditioned to be happy, gratified, and affirmed. Our aversion to negative emotions is certainly reflected in the language we use to talk about death and grieving. In her landmark book *The American Way of Death*, Jessica Mitford describes in eye-opening detail the playbook of the American funeral industry. She notes an intentional shift in terminology used by funeral directors in the last century. The word "corpse" was initially replaced with the word "body" and later was replaced with "remains." We now refer to "cremated remains" or "cremains" rather than "ashes." As soon as a word becomes too closely associated with death and pain, we replace it. It's a "casket" not a "coffin." It's a "mortician" not an "undertaker." We plan "services" not "funerals."[5]

Passed away. Departed. Eternally resting. These phrases and words are all designed to shield the heart from the reality of what has occurred. But what has occurred is death, a violent cessation. There is no way around it.

I found lots of creative ways over the years to ignore and numb the pain of death. When my grandmother died while I was in East Africa, I didn't tell any of my colleagues in the field. I basically pretended it had not happened until I got home. After my first miscarriage, I binge-watched three seasons of *Turn: Washington's Spies* (nothing like a little Revolutionary War drama to make you forget your troubles). After Rachel died, I became addicted to social media, constantly scrolling through the accolades and remembrances of her that people were posting. After my second and third miscarriages, I restocked our liquor cabinet.

I simply wasn't ready for the pain. To embrace my pain was to admit the hard truth that God was not who I thought He was. That my life was not what I thought it was. That *I* was not who I thought I was.

While traditional Jewish mourning practices stand in stark contrast to my ritual of Netflix binging and gin and tonic, I recognize the value of facing the sadness head-on, without any palliation. Pain is inevitable in life. This is a truth that is hard for privileged, healthy people like me to recognize. But once you recognize it, there is an immense freedom that buoys you up and out of the malaise of denial.

There was a strange sense of liberation that finally came in admitting that my carefully constructed life was going to be harder than I'd hoped or planned. I accepted that I was going to be caring for my aging parents and aunt without my sister. I recognized the fact that Tim and I might never have the large family we desired, and that if we kept trying, we would likely face more losses. I gave up on pretending, on trying to jury-rig what was broken. The pressure to deny or resist the reality of my circumstances was gone. I no longer needed to struggle to manufacture the life I'd once had, the one I'd hoped for and thought I deserved. I released control and allowed myself to feel truly disappointed. I could just let my life be what it was.

My mom, who grew up in Florida, used to issue a stern warning to me and my sister about riptides any time we'd visit the beach as kids. I've heard the only hope for survival if you get caught up in a rip current is to not struggle. Give up trying to swim against the current. Allow yourself to be taken out to sea, or tread water moving parallel to the shore. You'll reserve your strength and be able to swim back to safety when the tide has relented. Accept the reality of your circumstances.

Humans are remarkably resilient. Our eyes are designed to adjust to the darkness. This new night vision is almost like a super-power once acquired. But you have to keep your eyes open. You realize you can endure terrible things and still wake up in the morning. You can experience deep sadness and still love your friends, prepare a meal, make your bed, and watch a glorious sunset. Life doesn't have to be perfect to be good. You can reconstruct a new life even if it isn't everything you thought it would be. You realize you can experience the presence of God even in the absence of peace.

• • • • •

For several years leading up to my sister's death and the loss of my pregnancies, I'd begun to have some serious questions about my faith. Like so many who have walked through a season like this, I could feel my doubts casting a long shadow on every facet of my life. I had lost that sense of certainty that God's presence was real and active in my life. Where my previous automatic reflex in the face of challenge had been to pray and abide in the assurance of

His companionship, I now found that prayer was quickly followed by questions, then confusion, then disappointment with myself for being fickle and disappointment with God for being elusive.

I found it difficult to worship. Sometimes impossible. I'd stand in shadowy corners of the sanctuary watching my fellow church-goers raise their voices and their hands. I'd see their closed eyes and serene faces. I'd remember with muted sentimentality the days when I, too, could join the song, when His presence felt as close to me as the very breath in my lungs. I felt like the lamenter in Psalm 42, who remembers with longing what it was like to worship God in the temple even as he sojourns in a wilderness exile. I was thirsty for God. I was panting for God. I longed to worship, but I didn't know how.

Needless to say, by the time I was barreled over with bereavement, I'd all but lost the muscle memory of faith.

I have no idea why God, in His infinite wisdom, allowed my crisis of faith to collide so violently with the trial of grief. Sometimes I wonder if perhaps God allowed me to walk through this season because there is an upside-down kind of grace in knowing what it is to feel utterly without Him. As it turns out, that has been an unexpected and mysterious gift. It's a new vantage point for a person like me who grew up with God and the Bible and Jesus. I actually *do need* Him! Desperately! The feeling of His absence cultivated a beautiful longing in me and taught me not to take anything for granted. I never knew how much I wanted God's presence until I knew what it was to be without it.

In Matthew 13, Jesus tells the story of a man who found a treasure hidden in a field and, at once, sold everything he owned so he could buy the field. Jesus says that this is what the kingdom of heaven is like. I'd never understood this story until I felt bereft of God. I would have given up everything—my possessions, my health, my security, even my loved ones—to get Him back, to know the treasure of His presence once more, to feel the profound comfort of knowing He is as real and relevant as skin and bone, as bread and water. Maybe that's what the kingdom of heaven is like in its purest form: acute awareness of your need for God. Hunger. Thirst. Relentless longing.

• • • • •

"Shivah is intrusion."

I am sprawled out on my basement floor scribbling notes on a loose-leaf sheet of paper with a purple pencil I found on the piano. I am officially in quarantine, having just learned I'd had contact with someone who tested positive for COVID-19. Per CDC guidelines, I am to remain sequestered and away from other people until fourteen days past contact and monitor my symptoms. I can hear Jane's little feet pitter-pattering on the floor above me. The sound of running water and clinking dishes means Tim is cleaning up after dinner. They are close but far away, and I am missing the presence of my people in my life.

I am trying to make the most of the situation and take advantage of the quiet alone time to work on some writing. I've called my friend Shelley to discuss the practice of shivah. Shelley is Jewish and grew up in Israel.

I met Shelley six or seven years ago when her husband was a colleague at the relief organization where I worked. Shelley also has had a long career in international aid and global health.[6] She and I were good acquaintances for a long time. But when my sister died, we formed a fresh bond over the shared experience of bereavement.

Shelley has had an unimaginable encounter with grief. In one moment, her mom and her sister died in a horrific car crash. Her sister was nine months pregnant at the time. Ten days later, her grandmother, overcome by the loss, died as well. Shelley was just twenty years old at the time. Even as I type it now, the horror of it all takes my breath away. Shelley's experiences have taken her deep into the heart of shivah.

At the very start of the conversation, Shelley immediately begins talking about the quality of presence that is essential to the experience of shivah. What Protestant and Catholic funeral traditions cram into a brief visitation and funeral service, Jewish custom stretches out into a seven-day period. For those seven days of mourning, streams of visitors pour into the shivah home. The family of the departed is not once left alone, from morning until evening. She shares that people literally begin knocking on your door at 7:30 a.m. Visitors don't leave until it is time for you to sleep. She describes the guests as constant and intrusive, and I assumed that she would go on to say how exhausting and depleting that was for her. She shares, instead, how healing it was.

Shelley refers to shivah as a space utterly free of judgment or speculation. Familiarity and relaxed informality are of utmost importance. She laughs as she recalls one specific memory from her mother and sister's funeral in Israel. "All the Americans showed up in suits and dresses and pearls, like they were dressed for a job interview. My Israeli friends were all dressed simply and comfortably." No one dresses to impress. There is no effort on anyone's part to perform during shivah. The point is not to produce but to be present—present for the pain and present for one another. The mirrors are covered. There is no need to wear makeup or to mask the sorrow.

Shivah is a time of sheltered grief, where the family can focus exclusively on tending to their pain and processing their sorrow. Friends take care of the household tasks, prepare food, and provide for the family's needs. Visitors will bring simple dishes and gather around the family, sitting on the floor with them. Shelley says it's the physical presence that matters most. It's as if to say, "My words are hollow. My offering is not enough for this loss. But my body, sitting here next to yours, is good. It is enough."

Visitors look to the friends of Job as a tutorial on how *not* to conduct oneself in the shivah home. To offer advice or ask too many questions is seen as harmful and unloving. You intrude with your presence, not with your words, or theology, or trite platitudes. Silence is the default setting, and friends take cues from the mourning family on how to engage. If the family is sharing stories, visitors will also share stories. If the family is weeping, visitors will also weep. If the family is laughing, visitors will laugh along with them.

Shelley tells me that the friends who visit during shivah serve as a visual template for the years of joy you spent with your loved one and the years of grief that lie ahead of you. People from various seasons of life show up, reminding the mourner of the continuum of life. Shelley tells me this gave her courage to step into the next season, knowing that the presence of community will always be there.

In the immediate aftermath of loss, you may wonder how to continue on without the person you love, without the beloved who was such a strong pillar in your life. The future can feel impossible without them. The visitors of shivah are an answer to that question. You are surrounded by pillars of love and support, people who have been there for you in the past and who will be there for you in the years to come.

I am realizing as Shelley talks that for a mourner to reap the full benefits of shivah, she must submit to a series of conditions that I, in my most natural state, fight without fail. You have to allow yourself to depend on others, to truly need them. You have to accept help. You are not allowed to *host* the visitors of shivah. You must lay aside the desire to perform or impress during your time of bereavement and allow yourself to be weak and frail. This isn't a job interview or tryout for the grief all-star team. Shivah is a ritual for the broken, not the "best in show." You are *supposed* to fumble through grief. Once you accept these conditions, the presence of so many visitors is no longer a nuisance or a bother but, rather, a balm.

Shivah provides that next right step for friends who want to offer comfort but who are afraid to encroach on the bereaved, afraid of not knowing what to say or what to do. And it shows a mourner *how* to receive love. Shivah is indeed intrusion. Death must be trespassed upon. In shivah, fear is interrupted by friendship. Loneliness is interrupted by love. Pain is interrupted by presence.

• • • • •

We speak often of the nearness of God. We rarely speak of His farness.

We speak fondly of the peace He gives us. We only ever whisper of the violent rending and crushing He allows as part of life in this world. If we long for the peace that comes with His presence, we must also accept the melting and molding it can bring as well.

Shelley shares with me one additional aspect of Jewish mourning: the mourner's kaddish. This ancient prayer has been recited by the bereaved for centuries. The oldest version is found in a ninth-century prayer book, but it is likely older than that.[7] Rabbi Wayne D. Dosick writes, "The *Kaddish* is not a prayer for or about the dead. It is a doxology: a prayer of praise to God."[8] The text of the kaddish is as follows:

> Glorified and sanctified be God's great name throughout
> the world
>> which He has created according to His will.
>
> May He establish His kingdom in your lifetime and
> during your days,
>> and within the life of the entire House of Israel,
>>> speedily and soon;
>> and say, Amen.
>
> May His great name be blessed forever and to all eternity.
> Blessed and praised, glorified and exalted, extolled and
> honored,
>> adored and lauded be the name of the Holy One,
>>> blessed be He,
>> beyond all the blessings and hymns, praises and
>>> consolations that
>> are ever spoken in the world; and say, Amen.
>
> May there be abundant peace from heaven, and life, for us
>> and for all Israel; and say, Amen.
>
> He who creates peace in His celestial heights,
>> may He create peace for us and for all Israel;
>> and say, Amen.[9]

Shelley tells me that the mourner's kaddish is to be recited not only at memorials but also during every prayer service—morning, noon, and night—at the synagogue. Sometimes it is repeated several times within a single service.[10] By the time Shelley's mother and sister died, she knew the kaddish by heart. Judaism seamlessly integrates the practices of grief and worship into everyday life. She'd grown up hearing it, reciting it with others who had lost loved ones. She says, "The kaddish's frequent recitation in synagogue and in prayer books is a way to maintain an awareness and empathy toward those who grieve in our midst. And for mourners, the frequency with which it is recited provides permission to bring that grief into a welcome space of worship." From childhood, Shelley had been taught to weep and worship in one breath.

In grief, the kaddish tumbles out from memory. Shelley pauses and I can sense her smiling even through the phone. "It's almost like you vomit it out again and again until it's true. The kaddish puts you in your place." It puts grief in its place. It orients you to a bigger picture of God's sovereignty and faithfulness. "When you elevate God in your grief," Shelley says, "something transformative happens. You are lifted up as well. Your sights are lifted up."

The recitation of the kaddish is meant to be communal as well. In fact, technically, one should not say the kaddish or hold service without the presence of at least ten people, which is an acknowledgment that we were made to worship and to grieve in community.

Perhaps the role of the visitors of shivah is to stand in the gap when you feel that God is far off. In truth, the presence of others can feel a lot like the presence of God. Kate Bowler wrote, "At a time when I should have felt abandoned by God, I was not reduced to ashes. I felt like I was floating, floating on the love and prayers of all those who hummed around me like worker bees, bringing notes and flowers and warm socks and quilts embroidered with words of encouragement. They came in like priests and mirrored back to me the face of Jesus."[11]

In the same way, liturgy, a scripted prayer like the kaddish, bridges the gap between what we are feeling inside and what we trust to be true. The kaddish is the invitation that the psalmist speaks of in Psalm 42, out of the wilderness and back to the temple, back to the house of God.

I've come to believe that positive emotions or a sense of ease is not the best measuring stick for the quality of God's presence or the sanctity of our worship. Grief is fierce. God is fierce. And I never knew something could be fierce and good at the same time until I met God in my grief, until I *worshipped* Him in my grief. I never knew until now the peace that passes my understanding of privilege and prosperity. True peace, in the end, is a better way of being, not simply a better way of feeling.

And in the meantime, while we wait for that consoling salve, while we hold vigil until the violence of it all subsides with time and tending, shivah intrudes upon the anguish with presence and with praise. Grief sometimes requires some holy stand-ins: friends and neighbors when God feels absent, the scripted recitation of the kaddish when the heart to worship is hard to find. For now, this is enough. For now, this is what the kingdom of heaven is like.

CHAPTER 5

CASSEROLES

(BODY)

On this mountain the Lord Almighty will prepare
a feast of rich food for all peoples,
a banquet of aged wine—
the best of meats and the finest of wines.
On this mountain he will destroy
the shroud that enfolds all peoples,
the sheet that covers all nations;
he will swallow up death forever.
The Sovereign Lord will wipe away the tears
from all faces.

—Isaiah 25:6–8

I live in my body. My very existence is made possible by my physicality, this fleshy imperfect organism that is all my own. Dallas Willard once wrote that the body is "the original and primary place of *my dominion* and my responsibility. It is only through it that I have a world in which to live…It is only with and through this body that I receive a place in time and space and human history."[1]

Despite the miracle of our physical materiality, we all want to crawl out of our skin sometimes. We resent the confines of our bodies, disparage their shape or size, and fear their deterioration. Our devices allow us to deny our bodies' limitations and perimeters. We can mentally teleport ourselves to our preferred destinations at any time of the day or night. The digital world has disembodied us. Much of our lives is cognitively far-flung, rarely rooted in the physical space our bodies actually occupy.

Most *Homo sapiens* throughout history have had to think more about their bodies than privileged twenty-first-century Americans. In a world of scarcity, people have been necessarily preoccupied with what they will eat and drink and what they will wear (see Matt. 6:25). *My* body, on the other hand, is unusually well cared for. I have remarkably easy access to food when I'm hungry, water when I'm thirsty, warmth when I'm cold, and treatment when I'm sick. Vaccines and antibiotics have eliminated many common deadly illnesses. Because the resources needed to take care of my body are so readily available, it's easy to forget how crucial my physical well-being is. The placated body is easy to ignore. My good health in many ways feels like a foregone conclusion.

Rather, I am typically preoccupied with the parts of my being that I've deemed need more intentional tending, the things that are more susceptible to hurt or upheaval. My thoughts, my emotions, my spirit—these are the parts of me that are prone to harm, the parts that really matter, right? These are the parts that make me, *me*.

To compartmentalize the various aspects of our being is a flawed and sometimes fatal way to live. The body cannot be severed from the spirit any more than paint can be removed from a mural or melody can be extracted from a song. It is every bit as vulnerable to harm and needs just as much care as the spiritual and emotional life. A symbiotic relationship exists between my physical and non-physical selves, and when one is wounded, the other suffers. My health, physicality, thoughts, emotions, and spiritual well-being all coalesce to create *me*. They are all an essential part of my identity.

When I grieve, it is not just my heart that grieves. My body grieves too. Exposure to danger or loss sets off a series of physiological responses. Our autonomic nervous system and endocrine glands are designed to make us sweat, increase our heart and respiratory rates, relax our bowel and bladder muscles, and make more glucose when we are faced with a threat. This readies us for instant action, allowing us to combat the thing we sense is hazardous to our security. But the chemical messengers that trigger all these reactions often continue to circulate long after the perceived danger has passed. Many people report living in a state of heightened awareness and stress for many weeks after a significant loss. Some say it feels like panic.[2] Persistent, prolonged panic.

The most immediate physical symptoms of grief are fairly obvious: fatigue, digestive issues, muscle weakness, headaches, joint pain, and changes in sleeping and eating habits.[3] But research indicates that grief has the potential to have a hidden and long-term impact on our bodies. Studies show that bereavement is associated with elevated levels of cortisol, the stress hormone that is linked to cardiac risks, reduced immune function, and overall reduction in quality of life. Assessments of individuals in the first few weeks of loss report increased circulation of inflammatory cells. Altered heart rate and blood pressure are observed for months after a loss. In fact, an increased risk of mortality exists for individuals suffering from grief, up to 40 percent for a surviving spouse.[4]

Our physical bodies tell the story of what we have experienced emotionally, mentally, and spiritually. We may believe we can overcome the physical impact of trauma and loss by maintaining a certain level of mental fortitude or spiritual tenacity. But we cannot forever outsmart the physicality of grief and trauma. Not even our numbed-out, well-fed, drugged-up twenty-first-century American bodies are invincible.

Our ancestors seemed to understand the physical impact of grief. The Arthurian legends of the Middle Ages tell the story of Sir Gawain discovering the dead body of his brother Gaheris. The narrative says of Gawain that "his legs gave way, his heart failed, and he fell as if dead. For a long time he remained thus. Finally, he got up and ran to Gaheris, clasped him in his arms, and kissed him, but the kiss caused him so much sorrow that he fell again, unconscious, on the dead man's body."[5]

This extreme physical reaction to death was not unusual in medieval literature, nor was it uncommon in traditional mourning practices of the day. Many understood that encounters with grief and loss could overcome the body and initiate a physical reaction that was similar to death itself for the bereaved. In fact, grief was often listed as a cause of death in medical records from long ago.[6]

But as we learned from the Irish keeners, the church has at times pushed back on grandiose displays of physical and emotional turmoil. The canons of the patriarchate of Alexandria stated: "Those who are in mourning must remain in the church, monastery, or house, silent, calm and dignified, as befits those who believe in the truth of the resurrection."[7] A popular saying of Saint Bernard of Clairvaux from the Middle Ages was, "Non culpamus affectum, sed excessum" (We do not blame the emotion, but the excess).[8]

I wonder who in the church would have dared to scold or

charge with indignity the "excess" of our Savior Jesus in the Garden of Gethsemane, whose own anguish became so manifested in His physical body that His sweat became blood.

• • • • •

The morning after a miscarriage is hard to describe. The air feels heavy. Languid. Time stands still.

This was my first pregnancy. After a couple of years of trying to have a baby but not succeeding, we were shocked and elated to get a positive pregnancy test just a day before my thirty-third birthday. We spent the next month and a half dreaming and arguing about names and nursery decor, all the things nervous first-time parents do.

But during a routine ultrasound, our greatest fears were realized. At some point around the nine-week mark, the baby's heart had stopped beating and the womb had started to collapse. I had the doctor check a second time, and a third. There had been no outward sign that anything was wrong. No bleeding. No cramping. She held a box of tissues in front of my blank, tearless face. I was stupefied, but there was no doubt. Even my untrained eye could see it on the grainy ultrasound image. I was no longer pregnant. At least not exactly.

Miscarriage is a peculiar kind of death. It is a death that lives in your own body. The fatality is a part of you. A life has expired within the depths of your own anatomy and yet you go on living. A myriad of feelings ensue. Disbelief, guilt, shame, the feeling of being unclean, the feeling of being betrayed by your own body.

Due to the late nature of the loss, my doctor recommended a dilation and curettage process to remove the remains of the baby.

This would be safest for me and ensure a more speedy recovery and opportunity to once more try again. Trying. That's all that motherhood had been for me up to that point. Striving. Hoping. Losing.

The ultrasound and diagnosis were on a Wednesday. I asked for five days to pray for a miracle, so a follow-up ultrasound was scheduled for Friday, then another on Monday prior to the surgery, just to be sure. Yes, we prayed for a miracle, but my body, heart, and mind recognized instinctively that the baby was gone. We awoke that Thursday morning to a bright, sunny July morning that somehow felt gray and dull. The vibrant greens and yellows of the meadows and hillsides surrounding our house were muted outside our bedroom window. We both called out of work that day and lay in bed a long while, still and mostly silent, reorienting ourselves to the new reality that felt absent, most chiefly, of hope.

It's hard to know how to pass the time that first day after a loss so significant, the in-between of the death and the end. I felt like a walking corpse. The baby was still with me but was gone. When I finally had the energy to roll over and ask Tim what he wanted to do, he replied matter-of-factly, "We should probably go blueberry picking."

Right. Of course.

Old Orchard Creek Farm lies almost thirty miles down a winding, scenic mountain road from our house. We'd been talking about going for a few weeks, as it was full harvest season for blueberries. I pulled on an old T-shirt and we loaded ourselves into our Honda CRV, making our way through the soft Appalachian countryside.

We picked almost a year's supply of blueberries that day. We breathlessly climbed the hillside covered in old blueberry bushes and greedily filled our buckets, bees buzzing all around us and sweat trickling down our necks. I ate fistfuls of them as we picked, the sun beating down on us all the while. I carried that tiny, silent, still heart within me up and down the orchard rows until the colors of the land became vibrant again. When we got home, we washed the blueberries and laid them out on our kitchen table to dry. What we could not eat or make into pies that week, we froze and used in smoothies and berry cobblers for months to come. In our sorrow, we labored, gathered, and gleaned. And we were fed.

I will always remember the wisdom of my husband, that his first inclination after learning that my body was passing through the valley of the shadow of death was this: Let's go feed that body. Let's give it sunshine. Let's let it breathe.

• • • • •

If there is one mourning tradition that has remained largely intact in the Southern part of the United States, it's funeral feasts. Feeding the bereaved family is our ultimate grief ritual.

Growing up, I remember tables and tables of all kinds of casseroles, fried chicken, and deviled eggs being served after a visitation or funeral. There were apple pies, those wobbly Jell-O molds, and KFC biscuits arranged neatly in bread baskets to give the appearance that they'd been made at home from scratch. My mom would often cook and deliver meals to families who had lost loved ones. Beef pot roast, chicken casserole, and strawberry pretzel salad were her specialties. Even before the internet and the advent of meal train websites, a bereaved family could expect weeks of home-cooked meals to be delivered by neighbors, church communities, and coworkers. I'm not sure how it was all coordinated, but I do know this: a grieving family was never lacking in calories.

For the Southerner, there is very little symbolism or, frankly, nutritional consideration, in the food that is offered. We have a tightly held conviction that there is no sorrow that an abundance of butter cannot soothe. But historically and globally, the food served to the bereaved was symbolic, an art form in some ways. The symbolism provided a physical representation of sadness and helped to tell the story of the loss. Food played a precise role in the ritual of burying the dead and was often specifically designed to nurture the broken body of the bereaved.

Traditional Jewish practice calls for the meal of condolence, the first meal served after the burial of a loved one. The meal is prepared by neighbors and should include bread or rolls, the staff of life. It should also include hard-boiled eggs to symbolize the cyclical or continuous nature of life. Some note that the boiled egg is the only food that hardens the longer it is cooked, therefore serving as a reminder that a person must harden themselves in the face of grief.[9]

In days gone by in Switzerland, men would wrap lemons in their handkerchiefs and place them under their hats during funerals. After the ceremony, they would place the lemons on the graves as a way to symbolize the sharpness or bitterness of death and grief.[10]

Belgian funeral foods are traditionally black, devoid of color to symbolize the bleakness of death. Dark breads and cakes are served on black plates. Red wine is forbidden due to its color, so only white wine can be served. Fortunately, chocolate is allowed.[11]

In many countries, including England and Holland, it was customary to serve a kind of cookie or biscuit at the funeral service. The name or initial of the deceased was printed on the wrapper or imprinted directly on the cookie. Sometimes the cookies weren't even eaten by the mourners, and instead were kept for months and even years as a type of souvenir from the funeral, a token of remembrance of the dead.[12]

These cookies may have evolved from an older tradition of eating "corpse cakes." In Germany, corpse cakes were made of leavened dough by the woman of the house of the deceased. The dough would be left to rise on the chest of the deceased after he or she had been covered with a linen cloth. The dough was thought to absorb the qualities of the departed loved one. It was then baked and the virtues were passed on to the mourners who consumed the bread. Similar traditions, of placing food, drink, and even snuff on the body of the dead before serving it to friends and family, were common in Central Europe and Ireland.[13]

In the Greek Orthodox Church, it is traditional to make a mourning dish called *koliva* to be eaten on the ninth day of grieving. A typical *koliva* recipe calls for a mixture of wheat berries, sesame seeds, walnuts, almonds, raisins, and pomegranates. The dish is full of nourishing ingredients: protein, healthy carbohydrates and fats, and antioxidants. This tradition predates Christianity. The seeds symbolize the life of the departed; once they are consumed, the spirit of the departed lives on in the mourner's life and body. Christian tradition looks to the words of John 12:24 to affirm the ritual: "Very truly I tell you, unless a kernel of wheat falls to the ground and dies, it remains only a single seed. But if it dies, it produces many seeds."[14]

Fortunately, this tradition of eating at a funeral is one of the few grief rituals that, in many cases, has actually improved over time. In the Middle Ages in Europe, massive—and expensive—funeral feasts were expected to be provided *by* the bereaved *for* the community of condolers. It was considered shameful if you were too poor to provide a decent meal for the funeral guests.[15] But as time went on, the needs of the grieving family were considered to be the primary concern.

There have always been practical considerations connected to funeral foods. The traditional funeral pie of the Amish is the raisin pie because the ingredients aren't seasonal and therefore can be made at a moment's notice. It also travels well in the event that the bereaved friend lives some distance away.[16] Ham is a traditional component of any good British funeral tea. Ham leftovers can be kept by the bereaved family for several days and are appropriate to serve at any meal of the day. So common is the practice of serving this dish at funerals in Britain that the dead were often said to be "buried with ham."[17]

All these traditions acknowledge the physicality of what has transpired. They recognize that the bodies of the bereaved have taken a beating, and that proper dietary sustenance is needed to aid in restoration. The physical act of nourishment at least *begins* to address the relational amputation that has transpired in the death of a loved one.

Eating is often the first right step after loss. As the anguish rages inside you and all around you, the physical act of eating and drinking forces you back into the bodily rhythms and routines of everyday life. It's often the one "normal" thing you do in grief. In some ways, eating is an act of defiance. As food journalist Lisa Rogak writes: "There's no better way to prove you're alive…than by eating." She goes on, "When you're sharing a meal after a funeral, you're really poking a thumb in the eye of death. After all, with the simple act of eating, you're assuming you're going to need the fuel for the future you expect you're going to have…You can ask any caterer: most people eat a lot more food at funerals than at weddings. And that cuts across *all* cultures."[18]

• • • • •

I profoundly underestimated how powerful the physical sensation of grief would be. I felt like my brain had been put in a blender; like I had swallowed a bowling ball; like my skin was crawling with ants; like my heart, not just the metaphorical one but the literal one, had been launched into outer space.

Every significant loss I've experienced has been accompanied by some form of physical illness in my own body. Days after my grandmother died, I got food poisoning from a suspicious dish of baked fish and rice in Uganda. I became ill hours before boarding a long flight from Entebbe to Monrovia, Liberia. I was so pale and sweaty the flight attendant almost didn't let me get on the plane.

My body handled my first two miscarriages as well as could be expected, but by the time I had my third miscarriage the day after Ash Wednesday, I was well worn down by years of loss and infertility. Two days after I stopped bleeding, I experienced one of the worst stomach bugs of my life. I became so dehydrated that my heart began racing and my blood pressure plummeted. Tim had to rush me to the emergency room for treatment and I felt weakened and fragile for several weeks after.

During the three weeks leading up to my sister's death, I came down with a horrible virus that plagued me for almost a month. My fever soared to over 103, and the day she died I was still suffering from severe night sweats. In the hazy days that followed her death, my throat was raw and my ears were ringing. By the time we gathered for her funeral, I had lost almost fifteen pounds.

Because of these experiences, my memories of acute grief are profoundly somatic in nature. Bereavement to me *feels* like physical pain, a true ache in the bones and fever in the body. Loss is a memory I carry in my flesh, revisiting me at the cellular level. Nevertheless, in my pride, I assumed that if I could simply sort through the emotions I was having, then the body I inhabited would follow suit. I once again expected that the psychological aspects of my being were superior to the physical, that they could somehow hit some magical override button. Perhaps we are all recovering Gnostics, resentful of the ways our corporeity and empirical matter seem to hold us back and reveal the truth of how we are actually doing.

My friends saw what I could not see in the mirror. My body was losing the battle against grief. During a quick trip home in the midst of my sister's illness, my friend Christin delivered platefuls of pad thai and sushi. She sat with me on my couch and we cried and stuffed our faces, the first real meal I'd had in days. She tucked my baby into bed, and then all but tucked me in as well. The day after Rachel died, my friend Joni drove all the way to my hometown in Tennessee and took me out to my favorite local dive for breakfast where we ate eggs and chocolate chip pancakes dripping with maple syrup. My parents' neighbors delivered trays full of sandwich meats and cheeses, providing sustenance not only for us but also for the endless stream of close friends and family who had come in to offer support.

My mother-in-law from Wisconsin was down south during this time to help with the kids and she marveled at the distinct quality of Southern hospitality: pies, baked veggies drenched in butter, lasagna with endless layers, stews, barbecue and baked beans, cornbread casseroles, and all sorts of Southern delicacies showed up daily at our front door with a hug and warm words from church ladies, former colleagues, and old friends. I requested some of the recipes from those dishes, forever expanding my own repertoire of meals.

When I returned home after Rachel's death, I found that my

fridge and pantry had been stocked with milk, eggs, bread, leafy greens, yogurt, and cereal by my friends Lizzy, Emily, and Laurie—who also happened to clean my house from top to bottom while they were there. My friend Erin, with help from our church worship team, put together a tote full of healthy snacks to grab for the countless long road trips back to Tennessee that would follow in the months to come.

Pound by pound, fiber by fiber, cell by cell, my body re-formed and healed. And while the pies and pancakes served as an important and much-needed distraction from the pain of the initial loss, it was the long-term, habitual selection of real, healthy, nourishing foods that made the greatest impact. Nutritional psychiatrists note that serotonin, the ever-important neurotransmitter that mediates mood and inhibits pain, is primarily produced in the gastrointestinal tract. Whether or not you have good or bad gut bacteria facilitating this production plays an essential role in your overall health. Good gut bacteria comes from real, simple, and wholesome nutrition.

The brain requires a constant source of fuel (i.e., food), and if that fuel is high-quality, containing lots of vitamins, minerals, and antioxidants, the brain and its functional capacity will have some protection from oxidative stress, the damaging "waste" or free radicals that are produced when the body uses oxygen.[19] Simply put, the food you eat has a significant impact on your body, brain, and emotional fortitude.

I can honestly say that food, and I mean proper nutrition, brought me back to life after grief, almost as much as Scripture, prayer, and counseling. The daily ritual of scrambling an egg, of blending a spinach smoothie, of microwaving a hearty stew prepared by a friend—this moment-by-moment choice to be present in my body, to nurture my body, and to honor my body and all it had been through—was vital to my recovery. Meals became like liturgy to me. On the days when I could think of nothing else to do but cry and fret, I would remind myself, "There's one other thing to do."

Eat.

Author Janet Reich Elsbach writes, "The things we survive have one common thread: if we got through it, we must have eaten something." She goes on to describe the food offerings great and small that she received in the aftermath of her own sister's battle with cancer and eventual death:

> The bar of chocolate in an envelope, the bowl of hand-arranged seeds festooned with flowers, the homemade gingerbread people and the store-bought bagels, the pocket-sized gestures and the trunk-loads of food all made indelible impressions. Each one was a strand in the rope that tethered me to the land of the living and together they eventually pulled me to my feet again, altered but upright.[20]

• • • • •

Food is featured prominently throughout Scripture. It was an irresistible desire for the forbidden fruit that catapulted the world into chaos, and it will be a wedding supper that will mark the world's ultimate restoration. Feasts were embedded in the worship calendar of the ancient Israelites and were often held after long seasons of suffering. Jesus' miracles repeatedly involved the provision of food to hungry crowds, and the writer of Ecclesiastes lauds the savoring of food and drink as the antidote to disillusionment.

Why does food hold such a powerful and captivating place in our imaginations? Perhaps it is because the act of eating is experienced both by the body and by the soul. It is banal in nature, required for the preservation of our individual bodies and the species at large, but it is also extraordinarily pleasurable. Unlike many of the other mundane tasks my body requires of me to keep it alive, eating is truly enjoyable. God made food to taste good, to bring joy. Eating is both necessity and indulgence, survival and celebration.

The act of eating seems to be a first step in a person's reemergence from the valley of the shadow of death. After Jesus raised Jairus's daughter from the dead, He immediately instructed those attending her to give her something to eat (see Luke 8:53). Poor Eutychus, who fell to his death after falling asleep on the windowsill during one of Paul's long-winded sermons, was raised from the dead and straightaway headed back upstairs to share a meal with his fellow believers (see Acts 20:9–11). It was only after Jesus had provided a net full of fish and cooked up a savory breakfast on the shore that the disciples even recognized their resurrected Lord. The sharing of a meal together was the first act of true fellowship and communion they experienced with Jesus after that gruesome and traumatic day at the cross.

It is as if eating is proof of life. It shows that the survivor has chosen to go on living—to nourish her body so as to proceed, painful though it may be, into another day. It is also, perhaps, a choice to begin savoring once again the beauty and goodness that life has to offer. It is an act of faith that abundance still exists, even as you recover from an encounter with sorrow. Even if one is simply going through the motions, to eat is a holy act. So holy, Christ chose it as one of the church's most central acts of worship. Tish Harrison Warren writes: "Of all the things he could've chosen to be done 'in remembrance of him,' Jesus chose a meal. He could have asked his followers to do something impressive or mystical…but instead he picks the most ordinary of acts, eating, through which to be present with his people."[21]

We cannot subsist on sorrow alone forever. Sometimes the grief can be so all-encompassing that it seems to commandeer our most commonplace habits. Job said sighing became like a meal to him (see Job 4:24); and the psalmist said his tears were his daily food (see Ps. 42:3).

In stark contrast, Isaiah writes of a time of joy after a time of long suffering. On the Mount of Zion, after the Lord had brought justice to the earth and salvation to His children, the people feasted at a great banquet together. Not only did they eat meat, they ate only the choicest pieces. Not only did they drink wine, they drank the finest, aged wine (see Isa. 25:6). This holy replacement of sorrow for sustenance, of destitution for feasting, is part of the healing God brings. It is a physical, embodied restoration that God enacts in our lives. He not only addresses the emotional wounding; He resuscitates the visceral, material parts of our being as well. This, after all, is the true miracle of the resurrection—that both body and soul are brought back to life.

CHAPTER 6

POSTMORTEM PHOTOGRAPHY

(MEMORY)

*Are your wonders known in the place of darkness,
or your righteous deeds in the land of oblivion?*

—Psalm 88:12

One of history's greatest love stories is the marriage and partnership of Queen Victoria and Prince Albert. Victoria was the queen of the United Kingdom of Great Britain and Ireland from 1837 to 1901. She married Prince Albert when they were both just twenty-one years old, and together they had nine children. When Albert died at the young age of forty-two, Victoria was devastated. She spent her remaining forty years in strict mourning, living a life of seclusion and wearing only black clothing. She even had her late husband's sleeping quarters maintained as if he might come back from the dead at any moment. The people of the Commonwealth were fascinated with the queen's grieving process and many tried to model their own bereavement practices after hers. Never was it more in vogue to grieve than during the Victorian era.[1]

Helped along by the high mortality rates at the time, the funeral industry boomed. Undertakers facilitated a complicated system of bereavement rituals, thus enjoying huge profits. Funeral processions were to be elaborate and showy, with ornate hearses pulled by teams of regal horses. There were strict codes of fashion for grieving family members, particularly widows. Mourning jewelry, especially pieces crafted from locks of hair of the deceased, were very popular. "Mutes" were professional mourners hired to stand silently outside the door of the deceased and later lead the funeral march. They would carry poles draped in crape and wear black costumes along with a mournful expression on their faces.

The practice from that era that is most haunting to me is post-mortem photography, otherwise known as memento mori photography. *Memento mori*, which in Latin means "remember you must die," is a genre of art that includes any symbolic representation of the inevitability of death. The *danse macabre* was a type of memento mori, as was much of the jewelry produced in memory of deceased loved ones.

In the mid-1800s, photography was incredibly expensive. Rarely were family or individual portraits made. When a loved one died, particularly a child, postmortem photography created a way for that person's appearance to be forever commemorated. Many people's first and only photograph was one taken of them after they died.

The average life expectancy in America during the Victorian era was close to forty years.[2] Certainly, the prevalence of childhood illnesses and infant mortality brought that number down significantly. Imagine how difficult it would be if you had to rely solely on your own faulty memory to call forth the image of a loved one. The likeness of babies who succumbed to all-too-common childhood illnesses would often be forever forgotten. Postmortem photography offered grieving families a way to remember the deceased with precision and accuracy.

Postmortem photographs from the 1840s and 1850s were almost all daguerreotypes, in which images were rendered on a copper sheet burnished to look like a mirror. They were quite expensive, and were produced as three-dimensional objects enclosed in leather or ebony cases opened by a small, delicate handle. Daguerreotypes were intimate and tender, meant to be held in the hands and examined affectionately. They featured close-ups of the dead and captured the details of a loved one's countenance.[3]

Early postmortem photographs were excruciatingly realistic. Faces often bore the ravages of disease and death: pockmarks, sunken cheeks, and the gray complexion of dehydration. But as daguerreotypes gave way to the wet collodion process, photography became faster, cheaper, and more accessible. Artistic ingenuity expanded, and photographers sought new ways to make the dead look more lifelike. Eyes were painted on after development, cotton was stuffed in sunken cheeks, and bodies were even propped up to appear lifelike. One postmortem photographer from that era describes photographing an old man whose family had set him up in a big chair, put a pipe in his mouth, and lit the pipe. The family insisted he wouldn't look like himself any other way.[4]

Many times, the living would pose with the dead, sometimes creating a first and only family portrait. A group of siblings would be situated around a dead brother or sister, surrounded by the toys he or she liked to play with while living. Mothers would sit, holding their stillborn infants. In large family portraits, sometimes the only way to tell the living from the dead was to look for the person whose image was the sharpest. The requirement of long exposures for taking photographs meant that any movement on the part of the subject would create a blur. The dead do not move, and so their image would be strikingly clear.[5]

Medical historian Brandy Schillace writes, "The camera allows for a make-believe world, a place to pretend the dead are yet living, a space where the living and dead can both exist together. It freezes time—not as it is, but as you wish it were." This was a time outside of time, a reality outside of reality, where the dead weren't really dead, and the living forever embraced them.

• • • • •

While a postmortem photograph may freeze a loved one in time, the dead always seem to go on living in one way or another. "Death ends a life, not a relationship," Mitch Albom writes in *Tuesdays with Morrie*.[6] Our communion with the departed proceeds in the form of memory—memory that is obscured, creative, and now independent of the substantive influence of the person we are actually remembering. In many ways, death itself allows them to evolve and transform more than they did in real life. While the dead may be physically inert, our relationships with them move in a million different directions in our minds. The imaginary existence is always the most animated one.

In *A Grief Observed*, C. S. Lewis laments the danger of this new form of relationship:

Already, less than a month after her death, I can feel the slow, insidious beginning of a process that will make the H. I think of into a more and more imaginary woman... Won't the composition inevitably become more and more my own? The reality is no longer there to check me, to pull me up short, as the real H. so often did, so unexpectedly, by being so thoroughly herself and not me.[7]

Death tampers with our memories. It reconstructs the past. Grief usually alters our recollection of someone in one of two ways. It either renders all our remembrances completely nostalgic and unblemished, besainting the person we lost. Or it sullies our memories, making the past and the person out to be worse than they actually were, villainizing them unfairly. Death is absence. Sometimes, absence makes the heart grow fonder. And sometimes, absence makes the heart grow angrier. Sometimes, it does a little of both.

After my grandmother died, I'd spend weeks reminiscing about all the good times we shared together: the long picnic lunches under canopies of rhododendron up on Roan Mountain, the times she'd French-braid my hair, the Christmases when her van would pull into our driveway heavy-laden with homemade dolls and books and toy trains. Those weeks, she could do no wrong. There was never a kinder, jollier, more winsome grandmother.

In these moments, the grieving heart won't allow the head to think correctly or honestly about how difficult a relationship may have actually been in real life. To remember a lost loved one as anything other than a saint or a hero would feel disrespectful. In an attempt to honor their memory, you canonize them, placing them on a pedestal beyond the reach of reality.

But then there were other weeks, different weeks. At these times, I'd remember nothing but my grandmother's faults, the imperfections she carried simply by virtue of being human in this world. I would see the impact my grandmother's mistakes had on my own mother, and in turn, on me, and I'd become angry. It was an anger that could not be assuaged by my grandmother's real, live, perfumed presence laughing in our kitchen or planting roses in the yard. Grandmama, in all her wonderful human fallibility, was truly gone.

In the end, this cynicism was really a form of self-preservation, a strategy to protect my heart. It was on the days I felt the sting of her death most acutely that I assigned to her the villain's story. I made her into a person whose loss I could bear. Sometimes it's easier to be mad at her than to be heartsick that she is gone. The world has done a thorough job of teaching us to be angry. It has not done such a good job at teaching us to be sad. We sidestep sorrow habitually in our culture and go straight to the rituals of rage: judging, canceling, disowning.

Who she becomes in my memory is really less about her and more about me. I make her into a character I can manage in my grief. I wish more than anything that she, the real her, were here to interrupt me, to remind me of who she actually was. I wish she was here to help me feel all the feelings, complex though they may be—sadness, joy, anger, love.

C. S Lewis goes on to write:

Images, I suppose, have their use or they would not have been so popular...To me, however, their danger is more obvious...All reality is iconoclastic. The earthly beloved, even in this life, incessantly triumphs over your mere idea of her. And you want her to; you want her with all her resistances, all her faults, all her unexpectedness. That is, in her foursquare and independent reality. And this, not any image or memory, is what we are to love still, after she is dead.[8]

The dead are not the only ones we invent stories about in the aftermath of death. Grief can also alter our views of ourselves and the role we played in the story of our relationship. Sometimes, *I* am the villain. Actions and inactions from the past that used to be vague regrets transform into searing remorse and shame. There are times when I hate myself for not visiting my grandmother more. I am heartbroken that I didn't push her more to write her life story. I kick myself for not asking her to teach me to sew. I wish with every fiber of my being that I'd told her I loved her more.

She is gone, but I live on, carrying the impossible burden of all my regret, all my guilt, all the "I'm sorrys" and "I love yous" that went unsaid. As Emily Dickinson wrote:

> *Remorse is memory awake,*
> *Her companies astir,—*
> *A presence of departed acts*
> *At window and at door.*[9]

I live with the fact that my grandmother and sister will never have a chance to right the wrongs they've done. And neither will I. We are stuck, locked in a flat, achromatic snapshot of who we were in the moment of death. Meanwhile, my imagination runs wildly ahead in an infinity of color.

• • • • •

Some may wonder if I am going to write extensively about heaven or the resurrection in this book. After all, the hope of the resurrection, what N. T. Wright refers to as the "life *after* life after death,"[10] is the cornerstone of my life. I believe that the body of our dead Savior physically resurrected, literally, in real time and space. I believe His resurrection was the first fruit, the inaugural event of a coming kingdom in which we will all experience bodily resurrection. This is the foundational truth I've put my trust in. Jesus is alive and we will someday be alive eternally with Him. I am confident about this. On most days.

In spite of this, or perhaps because of my periodic doubts, I'm hesitant to speculate too much on the specifics of this hoped-for afterlife. I can't even guess what a resurrected body would look like, and I've never been totally comfortable when people try to tell me what my sister or my grandmother or my babies are supposedly doing in heaven right now. I bristle a bit when people tell me Rachel is looking down on me proudly, or when others say, "She's too busy worshipping Jesus to worry about us!" I tend to check out when I hear someone say that heaven gained three angels when my babies' hearts stopped beating.

Maybe some people are soothed by specifics. Personally, I find comfort in mystery. I'd rather the afterlife remain, at least in some part, an enigma. I like to think God is able to dream up far grander things for His children than I can. There are certainly things about the resurrection that we can know, or at least put our well-reasoned faith in. Maybe I'm strange, but I'm content for the rest to remain unfathomable, like seeing through a glass darkly.

The ancient Israelites wrote and spoke with relatively little elaboration about the place of death, known to them as Sheol, the netherworld. According to many Old Testament scholars like John Walton, the Hebrew view of the afterlife in many ways reflected the surrounding cultures of Mesopotamia. The netherworld was a place of chaos, a realm of disorder and darkness. For those cultures, the concept of the afterlife was not oriented around reward or punishment, heaven or hell. One did not wonder where one would go after dying. Sheol was the *only* possible destiny after death.[11]

Walton writes, "The ultimate death came when one was remembered no more."[12] The idea of being forgotten was a fate worse than death. For this reason, the ancients of that region placed an enormous amount of importance on having a strong line of descendants in order to assure being remembered. They strived to leave behind some esteemed legacy or robust inheritance to their children.

I came across Psalm 88 the year I went to Iraq and experienced my first miscarriage. It was a season when death felt real and close all the time. Here, the psalmist speculates on the afterlife:

Do you show your wonders to the dead?
Do their spirits rise up and praise you?
Is your love declared in the grave,
your faithfulness in Destruction?
Are your wonders known in the place of darkness
or your righteous deeds in the land of oblivion? (vv. 10–12)

Oblivion. The Hebrew word for it is *ne-shi-Yah*, and for some reason, I couldn't stop thinking about it after I read it. It's such an emotional word, one heavy with dread, vast and unknown. As I studied the word, I learned that Psalm 88 is the only place in all of Scripture where the term is used. Some versions translate the word "the land of forgetfulness."

It appears that the writer of the psalm is wondering if it's possible for the dead to see God's goodness and to praise Him for it. He wants to know if God even bothers to show His love and His glory in the place of the dead. Simply put, the psalmist seems to be asking two key questions here: When we die, will we forget God? And, perhaps more poignantly: When we die, will God forget us?

It's terrifying to think that we may be forgotten, erased by history, lost to God and to the people we love. How horrifying to be remembered wrongly, to be overtaken by someone else's poor memory. Isn't that why a photograph is so important? It captures an image, secures our existence. Perhaps in some ways, a photograph seems to save us from this oblivion, from the land of forgetfulness.

When I was in India, I lived in a compound that served as both a home and a school for HIV orphans and widows. One cool, rainy morning, a mother and her two children came to us for assistance. She was HIV positive, as was her youngest daughter. I've never seen such a sickly child. She was quite literally skin and bones, her countenance wasting away. Her eyes were dark and hollow, and no matter what I tried to do to cheer her or make her laugh, she was too weak even to smile.

I could probably mark that encounter as the moment I lost my idealism when it came to aid work. Our resources at the organization were stretched thin, and both mother and daughter were too sick to be admitted to our home. The director of the ministry wished them well and directed them to a list of medical resources nearby. Before they trudged off into the mist, I took the little girl's photograph. A quick click opened the shutter and affixed her gaze to me forever.

We heard the next day that the little girl had died that afternoon on her way home to her village. Her name was Ankita.

I wrestled with that moment for years, the moment we sent them away. Should I have done more? Could we have simply offered them a warm bed for the night and would that have made a difference? Could I have saved her? I was twenty-one and naive, a puffed-up do-gooder whose illusions of heroism had been dashed. It was the closest I'd ever been to death. I watched a little girl teetering on the edge of oblivion. It was like she'd fallen in before my very eyes.

I wondered what would become of her now that she was gone. Surely it wouldn't be long, a few decades maybe, before her memory vanished from the earth. By all accounts, she was an unnamed, unimportant village girl from a poor family that had become outcasts after the HIV diagnosis. In India, she was literally one in a billion. She would become a statistic, an integer added to the number of children in the world who die annually from AIDS. Who would care enough to remember her, in all her God-given specificity? Was my photograph all that was physically left of her? It was likely the only one ever taken of her.

If we all go to the land of forgetfulness in the end, there is but one hope: that God will remember us. Psalm 139:8 feels in many ways like a response to Psalm 88. It notes that even Sheol is not too far to be reached by the presence of God. That same passage tells us that God crafted each of us in our mother's womb, knit us together with remarkable particularity (see v. 13). Death cannot change this vital fact of our existence: we are made and loved by God. I might not know what eternity looks like, but I know that it belongs to me, that it is written on my heart. Even death can't deny me the dignity of eternity.

I learned later that the name Ankita means "marked." Indeed, she was marked by God. All human beings, no matter their status, skin color, virtues, vices, or length of life, bear the *imago Dei*. They are marked with His likeness, stamped with His image. That image transcends any image we seek to put out into the world, any legacy we want to leave behind, any effigy that someone else would falsely or mistakenly fashion of us. We are loved by God not because we are good or important or deserving or heroic, but because we are His. To simply exist is a miracle. What a noble purpose, in and of itself, to simply *be* as a child of God! He does not forget us because He cannot forget Himself.

In Isaiah, God compares Himself to a nursing mother, one whose love is fixed on a newborn child:

Zion said, "The LORD has forsaken me,
　　the Lord has forgotten me."
Can a mother forget the baby at her breast
　　and have no compassion on the child she has borne?
Though she may forget,
　　I will not forget you!
See, I have engraved you on the palms of my hands.
(49:14–16)

We all bear the mark of God. And, according to this passage, God bears the mark of us.

• • • • •

"Oblivion" is a word I clung to during my first miscarriage. It was the only word that seemed to describe the loss I was experiencing. Miscarriage is perhaps the only death you mourn in which you have no past with the loved one you lost. You have only an imaginary future. You grieve someone whose face exists only in your mind and whose name exists only as a hope.

Our culture has given us almost zero rituals for the observance of miscarriage. There is bleeding or an outpatient surgery and then it is over. You go home from the doctor's office with ibuprofen and instructions to rest awhile. In many cases, even close family members don't know a loss has occurred.

And what kind of existence did that child ever know? All it experienced was a life inside of mine. As Marilynne Robinson writes in her beautiful work of fiction *Lila*, "An unborn child lives the life of a woman it might never know, hearing her laugh or cry, feeling the scare that makes her catch her breath, tighten her belly. For months, its whole life would be all dreams and no waking."[13] For some, there will never be a waking.

If ever someone's existence felt lost in the oblivion, it is my unborn child's. You, sweet baby, were a part of me. I felt your presence to my very core, but I never saw you, never held you, never really knew you. Who are you and what is my love for you? Is it an apparition or an aspiration?

I can't explain it, but the mysterious nature of my child's existence troubled me for a long time. It was like I couldn't understand what had happened to us. I believed that my child was an image bearer of God, despite the brevity of his or her life. We had borne witness to that child's existence, but Tim and I felt all alone in that experience.

Maybe this is why many women stay silent, don't talk about this type of grief. The loss feels too abstract, too hard to name. Many have argued that the ubiquitous term "miscarriage" should be replaced by the term "pregnancy loss."[14] The meaning and etymology of the term "miscarriage" can sound inherently accusatory. The first definition that *Merriam-Webster's Dictionary* offers is "corrupt or incompetent management." Indeed, many women mistakenly feel that a lost pregnancy represents a failure on their part, that they did something wrong that led to the loss of their baby. In reality, we know that most pregnancy losses are due to chromosomal abnormalities, something the mother, and the father for that matter, has no control over.

I, however, am not quite ready to lose the term. A simple Google search of the word "miscarriage" turned up a definition that actually spoke to me in my place of hurt: "an unsuccessful outcome of something planned."

To me, miscarriage is an appropriate name, not only for a pregnancy loss, but for all sorts of losses. We make plans, live life with a person or a dream, and the future we hope for never comes to be. The outcome we anticipated is wrecked by an unforeseen cause, stolen incrementally or meteorically. We live in an alternate reality of the one we really wanted.

We *mis-carry* so many of our relationships, both in life and in death. Many do not come to full fruition. Relationships are a complex conglomeration of who a person is to us, what we hope them to be, and what we fear they will be. All relationships are riddled with expectations and disappointments, unrealistic optimism and unfair pessimism. Most folks are more flawed than we assume and are also more wonderful and valuable than we can ever know. No one will ever meet the grand heights of our expectations for them.

And most will surprise us with goodness more than once. Like most complex human experiences, relationships are a journey.

The problem with death is that it cuts the physicality of that journey short. We continue that journey with a ghost, who can't right wrongs, who can't evolve. Some ghosts are too big to fail; some do nothing but fail. Dead people transform into either gods or devils, angels or demons. Few find the in-between of what it means to actually be human.

Nor do we allow ourselves to be human. We beat ourselves up for things we said, or what we left unsaid. We spend the rest of our lives wondering, "What if?" Jerry Sittser, who in one evening lost his mother, wife, and daughter in one devastating car accident, wrote, "The difference between despair and hope, bitterness and forgiveness, hatred and love, and stagnation and vitality lies in the decisions we make about what to do in the face of regrets over an unchangeable and painful past."[15]

Learning to love people in death, it turns out, is a lot like learning to love them in life. No one is perfect. No one loves perfectly. To mourn well is to hold together in the space of your heart multiple complex emotions at once. Sadness, regret, anger, longing, nostalgia. All of these are holy feelings and must not be denied. Honoring the memory of the one you loved doesn't require you to idealize them. They don't need your patronization. To honor them means to love them because of, and sometimes in spite of, who they really were. And to honor your own sorrow, you must love and accept yourself no matter the mistakes you've made.

One of the most powerful things about the gospel is that it teaches us people do not have to be perfect to be loved, cherished, and grieved when they are gone. And *I* don't have to be perfect to be *allowed* to grieve.

It is a gift to bear witness to the life of another. When I look back on the lives of my sister and my grandmother, there are moments that bring me pain. But there are moments I would freeze in time if I could. I'd give anything to go back and feel my grandmother's long fingernails combing through my hair. I'd give anything to be a kid again, stuck in the backseat of our Chevy Caprice, crammed in with our suitcases and my sister on one of our long road trips up to the Roan or out west. I'd give anything to go back to that rainy spring day when I told Tim we were miraculously pregnant; the smell of spring blossoms was drifting in through the open windows and we were wide-eyed and unbelieving and hopeful all at the same time.

Life doesn't exist as a snapshot. It's more like a movie reel, moving from frame to frame, from joy to sorrow over and over again. Time takes us all to death at some point. Photographer Susan Sontag wrote: "All photographs are memento mori. To take a photograph is to participate in another person's (or thing's) mortality, vulnerability, mutability. Precisely by slicing out this moment and freezing it, all photographs testify to time's relentless melt."[16]

Death is voracious. It will take every inch you give it. It will rob you of the past, bereave you of your fondest recollections if you allow it. Memories that once brought joy can be transformed into tools of torture. Photographs from holidays, weddings, and birthdays are tarnished with sorrow, and even shame. You know that you'll never have the chance to relive the happy moments. There's a strange embarrassment at feeling like you had no idea what was coming, like you'd been caught off guard, like in all those happy moments, you should have known better or been better prepared. Death makes us feel like we've been hoodwinked. It's the greatest heist in history.

We must fight with all our might to maintain the joy of our memories. In reality, the past and the present are all we actually have. The future is never promised to us. As my brother-in-law, Dan, says, "It exists in my imagination." Death steals from me what I never fully possessed to begin with.

Perhaps in its very name, memento mori photography serves as a warning to us, a clarion call to be present in the moment for all that it is, the good and the bad, the beautiful and the hard. Cling to reality. Reminisce rightly. Because no matter our striving, our preserving, our imagining and reimagining, all things pass. All things are fleeting. Death is the common denominator of our shared fragility.

Memento. Remember.

Mori. You must die.

Remember.

CHAPTER 7

SYMPATHY CARDS

(WORDS)

Gracious words are a honeycomb,
sweet to the soul and healing to the bones.
—Proverbs 16:24

Since almost the dawn of time, philosophers have been arguing about the nature of language, namely, its inadequacy. René Descartes claimed that language was misleading because of the personal judgments and assumptions that are inherently built into it. Thomas Hobbes said that words were the "money of fools"; as much as we try, we cannot buy truth with them. David Hume thought that language deludes us; what we assume are ideas are merely illusions or fiction.[1]

I'm no philosopher. Frankly, I'm a writer and I still feel a deep frustration with the inadequacy of words. We all do at the street level of life, from unresolved office spats, to recurring spousal disputes, from explaining the concept of God to a toddler, to trying to express the depth of one's affection to a lover. The insufficiency of language is perhaps never more acutely felt than when death strikes, when you desire nothing more than to comfort a friend, but you simply don't have the words.

"I just don't even know what to say right now." It's a phrase I've heard many times in my life. I've heard it uttered by fellow aid workers as we stared out into fields of debris in the aftermath of a hurricane or flood, hands over our gaping mouths. I've seen it appear in texts on my phone as I informed friends that I would not be having a baby this year after all. I've heard it choked out through sobs as loved ones learned of my sister's death. I've said it myself, to a friend after she received a stage four cancer diagnosis in the prime of her life. To a colleague who had lost his wife.

This frank honesty is refreshing in some ways and names outright how deficient we all are in the face of tragedy. I've never minded it, never held it against anyone for saying it. If there's one thing that we all have in common, it's that grief makes us all novices. Death is not natural, and its dialect is foreign to us.

There are plenty of phrases we utilize as placeholders in an attempt to communicate the inexpressible. We "hold space," "send love and light," and relay "thoughts and prayers." Many people turn to customary expressions of worship during times of grief. They immediately revert to the hope we have in the life to come, to the comfort of knowing God's ways are higher than ours, and to the anticipation of the "sweet by-and-by." But these invocations of gladness have always felt mismatched to the moment for me. Phrases and sentiments that once felt like a familiar buoy of hope can feel like betrayal when leveraged at the wrong time.

Almost eight years ago, I was visiting a refugee resettlement camp in Uganda. Our teams were providing livelihood supplies to Congolese refugees who had fled their homeland and crossed the border. As our Land Rover rattled down the rutted red dirt roads of the camp, I stared out the window at crude hut after crude hut, family after family that was eking out an existence in this wilderness.

Many people shared with us stories of their flight from Congo. Most were missing family members. The stories of refugees were all too familiar: a little boy who had been captured by a rebel militia, a mother who had been raped and shot, a little girl who'd fled into the jungle and had to be left behind so the rest of the family could escape in time.

We bumped confidently along down the road while the stereo system blasted a popular worship song. The song was praising God for being the defender of the weak, the One who lifts up the needy on the wings of the eagles. Really? Defender of the weak? What about these people? Who defended them in their time of need? What comfort have You offered them, God?

Similarly, after my sister died, I'd cringe to hear the song "Christ the Lord Is Risen Today." For me at the time, that song posed cruel questions followed by shouts of acclamation that left me feeling hollow and gutted: "Where, O death, is now thy sting? Alleluia!" and "Where's thy victory, oh grave? Alleluia!"

I knew exactly where death's sting was. I'd just put my only sister in a box and laid her in the ground. That felt an awful lot like a victory for death to me.

Sometimes, something that is true isn't the *whole* truth. Never is it more important to tell the whole truth than in times of deep sorrow and confusion. If we are going to speak to the hope of a situation, we must also speak to the pain of it, the agonizing sorrow of the loss.

It is Scripture itself that offers us an alternative language in the midst of our confused sorrow. This language is called lament. Biblical scholars note that laments make up nearly one-third of the psalms, and the prophetic books of the Old Testament are brimming with them. Jesus Himself laments over the wayward state of Jerusalem (see Matt. 23:37–39). Akin to the death wail, the words offered in lament are untamed and brazen. They challenge platitudes and dismantle our cheery charades. They name unequivocally what is wrong and broken in the world.

Lament does not deny hope. Rather, lament tests hope's mettle, summons it into the darkness, where it actually belongs. Author, singer-songwriter, and theologian Michael Card writes, "Lament is not a path *to* worship, but the path *of* worship."[2] When we operationalize the severe and painful language of lament, we stand in agreement with God. We affirm with Him that suffering mars our existence and death is brutal and unnatural. We declare that evil is in opposition to His plan and that sin is the great enemy of our flesh and spirit. We assert that love is divine and divinely bestowed, and the loss of it is cruel and unusual. What is worship, if not to stand in agreement with God in truth, in joy, and in sorrow?

• • • • •

I've never been totally comfortable with the word "sympathy," much less with an entire genre of cards dedicated to the concept. To me the word has a patronizing connotation. No one likes the idea of somebody *feeling sorry* for you. Having someone's sympathy, to me, indicates that a weakness or vulnerability is present on my part. It makes me feel like I'm a bother or a problem that needs fixing.

Maybe it's the cards themselves that make me feel uncomfortable. Most sympathy cards depict tranquil scenes in soft-hued pastels. They often portray the halcyon landscape of a Thomas Kinkade reality: gently rolling hills, pastoral homesteads, serene seashores, and kindly creatures such as deer, birds, and butterflies. Also flowers. Lots of flowers.

These images stand in stark contrast to the actual experience of a loved one's death. Death feels nothing like a walk in the park or a peaceful stroll on the beach. But I get the point. Why add insult to injury? When expressing sympathy, it seems most sensitive to convey your message with an air of calm and placidity. But it hasn't always been that way.

The genre of the sympathy card is an outlier in the greeting card industry as a whole. After all, almost every other category of greeting card exists to recognize celebratory occasions: birthdays, graduations, weddings, and holidays. While *letters* of sympathy, congratulations, and friendship have been written and delivered for ages, greeting cards did not emerge as a cohesive industry until the mid-nineteenth century. Christmas cards, which originated in England as special drawings with messages designed to spread Christmas cheer, initially dominated the trade. These were lithographed, printed, colored by hand, and produced up to a thousand at a time, though this number quickly increased as the business of merrymaking took off.[3] Birthday and Easter cards followed shortly thereafter.

Sympathy cards were slower to follow. In fact, the first sympathy cards ever to be produced were sent *by* the bereaved to the community to announce the death of a loved one. "The cards were very somber looking," writes Hallmark archivist and historian Sharman Roberts. Some included artwork and simple poetry. "You would have known the minute you received a sympathy card that the message was death. All used lots of black—or maybe an engraved image of a mourner or tombstone. The envelopes were edged in black. There would be no mistaking the intent of the card."[4]

Brandy Schillace notes that in these early death notices, people did not "pass on." They died. The announcements named with little delicacy the grave reality of the situation. But that directness did not last long. She cites a card sent in the late nineteenth century that reads: "And though the body *moulders* here, the soul is safe in heaven." A mere ten years later, in the early twentieth century, another card with the same poem was sent, with one slight alteration: "And though the body *slumbers* here, the soul is safe in heaven." In the span of just a decade, the dead went from decaying to simply sleeping.[5]

The use of euphemisms continued to expand along with the sympathy card business. Sympathy cards as we know them today, sent *from* condolers to the bereaved family, began to emerge in the 1910s. They were originally simple and utilized muted pastels for coloring. Most offered words of comfort in the form of short, rhyming poems that expressed fondness for the departed, hope for the life to come, and love for those in grief.[6]

Few if any cards now use the word "dead" or "death." They might mention suffering, hardship, or trial. But most refrain from explicitly naming the occasion for the sending of the card. Images on cards are usually nature-themed, portraying deer, seashells, flowers, trees, or sunsets. Religious imagery such as a cross, angels, or praying hands is also common.

I suppose most people prefer that their sympathy cards strike a happy medium between the forthright and the circuitous, the somber and the reassuring. Perhaps the aesthetic history of greeting cards reflects our increased reticence to overtly name the tragedy that has occurred. It showcases our fear of doing or saying the wrong thing and highlights an underlying assumption that the best thing you can do for a mourner is to soften, reframe, or even deny the new reality in which they are living. What we are tempted to do for ourselves in the face of tragedy—numb, ignore, harden ourselves—we are tempted to do for others. But this is misguided mercy. And many times, it's the easy way out.

• • • • •

Meghan O'Rourke, who writes about grieving the loss of her mother to cancer in her memoir *The Long Goodbye*, bemoans the loss of rituals in our society. She writes, "The disappearance of mourning rituals affects everyone, not just the mourner. One of the reasons many people are unsure about how to act around a loss is that they lack rules or meaningful conventions, and they fear making a mistake. Rituals used to help the community by giving everyone a sense of what to do or say."[7]

I know from experience that it's a daunting endeavor to offer condolences to someone. But I never realized how much work it was to *receive* condolences, especially as a well-curated introvert. By default, I like to be left alone. It's important to me for people to think I'm managing the ups and downs of life with competence and tenacity, and it's easiest to maintain this persona by keeping people at arm's length. Simply listening to someone's offer of comfort means having to show up emotionally to hear it and accept it.

It requires you to admit struggle. This, I suppose, is all part of the grief work. I guess it's the labor of being loved.

But there are a few things that make that labor a bit more manageable. The truth is, people have said some strange and unhelpful things to me in the aftermath of my losses. Some of them were downright bizarre. But people have also said valuable things, beautiful things. They have shown up and offered words that filled me up rather than drained me. I've tried to sort out what makes a statement or sentiment helpful and what makes it hurtful. What is the "x factor" that makes a condolence particularly…condolatory?

Shortly after the start of the pandemic, I received an email from an acquaintance whom we'd bought a piano from a few years prior. It was a short email, in which he simply stated that he was thinking of me because it must be so hard for me to hear people dismissing COVID-19 as "just the flu" when my sister had died after contracting the flu. He told me he was praying for me. Something about that email made me feel so seen. He acknowledged how random and painful the triggers of grief can be, even a year or more later. He noticed what no one else had noticed.

Four months after my sister died, Hurricane Dorian ravaged the Bahamas, and I went down to the island nation as part of a team to set up a disaster response. A colleague named Hannah, whom I'd met only in passing, was part of the team. One evening, in the midst of the chaos of the response, she pulled me aside and told me that she, too, had lost a sister when she was younger. She didn't go into great detail, but she acknowledged how complex and life-altering it is to lose a sibling, and she told me that I was not alone.

Sometimes, when people learn of your loss, they want to connect with you in that holy, hollow space that is grief. And the easiest way to relate is by sharing about a similar experience. There were quite a few times in the weeks after my sister's death that I was cornered at the office, the grocery store, or at church by people who initially approached me to offer sympathy, but then went on to share in exhaustive detail their own grief story. By the end of the conversation, they were in tears and I was trying to comfort them. I don't always mind stepping into another person's pain with them, but in an attempt to show understanding, people often inadvertently ask the bereaved, still fresh off of a loss, to shoulder more than they are already carrying.

What Hannah offered me, quite literally in the midst of a disaster, was a glimpse of her own sorrow, as a show of solidarity and a reminder that I wasn't alone. She didn't do it in such a way that required me to carry anything or that centered herself in that moment. Rather, she reminded me that she was there to walk alongside me if ever I needed it.

The week after my sister died, Tim and I drove home to North Carolina in a stupor, completely disoriented by what we'd experienced over the last four weeks and overwhelmed by all the arrangements yet to be made for the funeral. Our friends Lizzy and Graham reached out to us: "Just let us know when you want us to come over." They said they'd get a babysitter, bring food, and hunker down with us to talk for as long as we needed. The night they came over was the first night in almost a month that I'd felt myself take a breath, as Tim and I were able to sit at a table with friends who cared deeply for us, and talk, curse, yell, laugh, and cry for as long as we needed.

Gifted condolers follow the protocols of sitting shivah by taking cues on how to *be with* the griever *from* the griever. Believe it or not, a bereaved person doesn't always want to cry. Sometimes they want to laugh. Sometimes they want to scream. Sometimes they want to sit in silence. Sometimes they want to talk about death and some-times they want to talk about other things (because our lives are so much more than the grief we are experiencing!). Lizzy and Graham made space for all these emotions and offered their unconditional presence for everything we were feeling.

The most impactful condolence I received came to me from my boss at the time. As I was leaving the office to drive back to Tennessee for my sister's funeral, I nearly broke down in his office, completely wrecked by what I was stepping into that weekend.

"How am I going to do this?" I asked him and began to share how overwhelming the funeral planning had been, how nervous I was to deliver the eulogy, and how devastated I was for my parents, my brother-in-law, and my niece and nephew.

He listened intently and then paused before offering a humble word of advice.

"God will help you."

"What?"

"God will help you."

It wasn't a theological treatise. It wasn't an explanation of what happened or why it had happened. It wasn't a promise that every-thing was going to be okay. It was a simple offering of wisdom, coming from a man who had seen his fair share of suffering. It was a statement of elementary truth to which I could cling. I was not alone. God was not absent. While He might not alleviate my pain, He would guide me as I navigated my way through it.

That humble word of wisdom carried me through the funeral and the months to follow. It didn't answer every question or soothe every fear, and it wasn't a map with precise directions out of the wilderness of grief. But it was a compass, a true north.

To feel seen. To connect in simple solidarity. To be offered unconditional presence. To be given a word of wisdom. What each of these friends offered had one thing in common. Love. Their condolences were not about them, but about me. True, deep love need not embellish itself with eloquence or well-rehearsed rhetoric. Though it may at times be offered timidly, clumsily, or imperfectly, real love never fails. Never.

• • • • •

When my sister died, hundreds of sympathy cards, letters of condolence, and notes of encouragement came in from all over the world. There were stacks and stacks of them, from every corner of the US, from Japan, Australia, the UK, and the Netherlands. My parents devoured them in the weeks that followed her death, reading every word and drawing comfort from the love and prayers being offered.

I, however, avoided those cards like the plague.

The truth is, every ritual of mourning has the potential to send you deeper and deeper into the reality of your loss. To read those cards would have been to acknowledge afresh that she was in fact gone. Receiving a sympathy card means that someone you love has died. I was still not ready to fully accept that she had died.

Finally, just before the one-year anniversary of her death, I decided that it was time. After visiting my parents one weekend, I packed up my car and placed the box brimming with pastel-colored envelopes carefully in the backseat next to my sleeping toddler. Once I got home, I began to read. Not all at once. But slowly, a few at a time, whenever I found the strength to do so. It took me eight months to read them all.

The cards that were sent to us weren't especially unique or extraordinary. Many were typical sympathy cards, imprinted with the customary tranquil landscapes, florals, and crosses. Yet, they were in many ways profound. This was because so many of those who sent cards had the courage to offer their personal words to us in our time of mourning.

Most of the letters began in a similar fashion. The writer acknowledged how imperfect and inadequate their words would be. Many stated how foolish they felt even trying to extend comfort. But, as one person wrote in their card, words were all they had to offer.

After reading the first dozen or so, I resolved to approach that box of cards not with a spirit of vigilance, wariness, or cynicism. Cynicism is a cruel companion in grief. It leaves you feeling nothing but smug and empty. I silenced the voice inside that said: *This person has no idea what I am going through*, or *What do they even know about my sister?* or *How dare you write about hope at a time like this!*

Instead, I decided to try to approach the cards and letters with a spirit of trust and curiosity. With curiosity as my companion, I discovered so much extraordinary beauty in those cards. I felt seen, like an army of condolers was bearing witness to my pain, not in a way that was voyeuristic, but with reverence, respect, and deep empathy. I found words of wisdom; insights that reoriented me around the truth. I felt camaraderie, as many people shared that they also had experienced catastrophic loss and had survived. Mostly, I felt love, geographically far-flung, yet mysteriously close and intimate.

Perhaps sympathy cards have been inaptly named. I wonder at times if they should be called *empathy* cards. "Empathy" as a term has its own complex and ever-evolving history. The concept didn't exist in the English language until it was introduced by the

American psychologist Edward Titchener in 1909 as a translation of the German *Einfühlung*, which means "feeling into."[8] Empathy involves a much deeper level of emotional engagement than sympathy. Empathy moves from the spectatorship of sympathy toward actual participation. You feel another person's pain as if it were your own.[9] Inherent in empathy is risk, the chance that you, too, may experience the waves of sorrow churned up by grief. But few good, beautiful, and meaningful things in life don't involve some level of risk. Love is a risk. Condolences are a risk.

When I look back on all the sympathy cards I received and the condolences I was offered, I truly feel that friends and strangers alike took the risk of entering into my sorrow with me. One card we received from Amy in Raleigh was engraved with a simple swirling, silver design and was imprinted with the words: "There's no map for this kind of loss." On the inside she had written a simple note: "The Lord draws near to the brokenhearted."

True. There is no map. But her words became my compass.

· · · · ·

We've lost our way with words when it comes to sorrow. In recent years, people have rightly named how hurtful and damaging fictitious platitudes can be. We've recognized that you can't simply explain away suffering or provide a theological elucidation to bring someone to the other side of grief. We've emphasized the importance of mere presence and encouraged the use of supportive silence. This was needed.

But I'm afraid the result is that now, anyone who would dare to offer condolences does so at their own peril. People are afraid. They fear saying or doing the wrong thing and being shut out, so much so that sometimes they fail to show up at all. It's uncomfortable enough to simply *be* around people who are suffering. Fear of rubbing salt in the wounds with an ill-timed word is enough to make many avoid the bereaved entirely. This has been one of the hardest parts of grief for me. I hate feeling like I'm putting people in an awkward position. I *hate* being the elephant in the room.

To be honest, sometimes the grieved just want words, imperfect though they may be, to fill the void. Death itself is enough of a hush. In their book, *There Is No Good Card for This: What to Say and Do When Life Is Scary, Awful, and Unfair to People You Love*, Kelsey Crowe and Emily McDowell write, "All of our difficult times involve some degree of shame, fear, and loneliness. At times like that, we don't need anyone to impress us or skillfully talk us out of our pain. We mostly just need the kindness that compels anyone to try."[10] To me, you can say almost anything, and as long as it's said in kindness, I can receive it as an offering of love. I will say that without a doubt, absence is more painful than someone's imperfect presence, and silence is more wounding than someone's awkward attempts at offering comfort. Love covers a multitude of imperfect words.

The latter part of Romans chapter 8 is a passage about present sufferings and future hope. We join with creation in groaning, as fervently as a woman in labor, for physical renewal and the redemption of our bodies (see vv. 22–23). We have been given the first fruits of the Spirit, but the full harvest of the kingdom is yet to come. In this mysterious space of the already-but-not-yet, Paul recognizes an important fact: We do not know how to pray. Words escape us.

But once again, we find an example of love's unfailing tenacity. God does not leave us alone in our weakness, but rather gives His

Spirit to join us in our groanings. The groans of the Holy Spirit transcend language, uttering hopes, desires, requests, and sorrows that are "too deep for words" (Rom. 8:26 ESV). As this sacred translation occurs between the human and the divine, we experience the unfailing love of a God who doesn't require sanctimonious elocution in order to hear us. As it turns out, groans seem to be the holy language that God speaks.

Love. Lament. Empathy. Hope. Presence. More than eloquence or poise, these are the competencies that make you fluent in the language of condolence.

During a typical year, sympathy cards make up 6 percent of all greeting cards sent for everyday purposes.[11] But in April 2020, that percentage drastically increased. While most of us were aware of pandemic shortages of toilet paper and hand sanitizer, retailers were dealing with short supplies of another item: sympathy cards. In hard-hit areas like New York and Florida, shelves of sympathy cards in drugstores and grocery stores were empty. One online greeting card retailer noted that she normally sells six sympathy cards per month. In April 2020, she sold 275.

When a pandemic deprives us of our typical ceremonies and customs, we cling to the few safe practices that remain. We may not be able to gather for funerals or even deliver meals, but we can send a card in the mail. We may be robbed of our rituals, but we will always have our words. No plague or pestilence, no upheaval or uncertainty can steal the love and sympathy we have for one another. Ann Peterson, who designs cards and sells them online, said her best-selling card in those early days of the pandemic bore the image of an angel with her forehead pressed into her arm.[12]

As if we were joining our imperfect voices with the heavenly groans of celestial beings.

CHAPTER 8

WEARING BLACK

(CANDOR)

I have sewed sackcloth over my skin
and buried my brow in the dust.

—Job 16:15

D oes this look like a cocktail dress?"

I was standing awkwardly in a dressing room in Belk. My friend Christin had graciously agreed to go shopping with me to look for a dress to wear to my sister's funeral. Christin is a good friend, so she redirected the question back to me. "How do *you feel* in the dress?" she asked me.

I stood on my tiptoes and cocked my head, peering in the mirror. It was one of those oft-repeated, idiosyncratic movements, something I'd seen my sister do a hundred times growing up whenever we'd put on dress-up clothes or go shopping together. Two sisters, both short in stature, both eager to elongate our bodies when trying on clothes, thoughtfully assessing our appearances. "It looks great!" she'd say as I sucked in my tummy and pulled at the neckline. "It's totally your color!" I'd say as she pursed her lips and pinched her cheeks. Halloween costumes, first-day-of-school outfits, prom dresses, wedding dresses. This time she was not behind me in the mirror. I folded my arms across my chest, wanting, inch by inch, to cover myself and disappear. I was shopping for a funeral dress without her. Because it was her funeral.

The particular dress in question did, in fact, look like a cocktail dress, so I moved on to the next option. Every dress I'd picked out that day was either gray, beige, or blue. For some reason, I felt uncomfortable with the idea of wearing black. I'd always thought wearing black at a funeral was a bit passé, an outdated formality. I didn't want to come off as being too dramatic, or like I was wearing a costume. And I didn't want to bring down the mood.

The mood, Amanda? The mood? At a funeral?

Christin was deeply convicted that I should feel permission to wear whatever I wanted to my sister's funeral, and she dutifully reminded me of this five to ten times during the course of our shopping excursion. The problem was, I didn't really know what I wanted to wear. I was still overly preoccupied by how I was coming across to the world. I wanted people's sympathy but not their condescension. I wanted people to think I was coping well.

In the end, I chose a tasteful navy-colored dress. Not too dark, not too cliché, not too bleak, not too theatrical. I thought that navy was moderate, a good blend of somber but serene.

Navy. It epitomized subdued sorrow. Looking back, it was the wrong color choice. How did I feel in the dress? Maybe I should have asked myself simply, *How do I feel?* I was not feeling subdued. I was not feeling serene. Everything was dark and bleak.

I should have bought a black dress.

As we were paying at the register, I turned to Christin with a brave smile and said the thing every well-meaning bride says to her bridesmaids who are being forced to wear something ridiculously floofy for her big event: "This is a classic dress. Super versatile. Definitely one that can be worn again and again." She smiled back and nodded positively. Like I said, she's a good friend.

The truth is, I haven't touched the dress since the funeral. It's still hanging in the closet of my childhood bedroom in my hometown.

• • • • •

I'm not the only person who has struggled to know what to wear in the days and months after a significant loss. The history of mourning dress in the Western world is tightly woven into the histories of industry, manufacturing, fashion, religion, and socioeconomic mobility.

"Widow's weeds"—drawn from the Old English word "waed," which means "garment"—trace their origins back to the early days of the Christian convent. Nuns wore shapeless robes of black, gray, and brown to display their chastity, humility, and rejection of vanity. Likewise, widows wore the same to show their grief and rejection of a joyful, frivolous life.[1] Some believe that the custom of wearing black originated from the ancient notion that evil spirits would hover over a corpse. Black was worn by the living to make themselves inconspicuous and therefore unbothered by the menacing spirits.[2]

Styles, trends, and various iterations of the mourning dress for both men and women—including robes, sashes, veils, hoods, hats, and wimples of white and black—emerged and declined throughout the Middle Ages among the aristocracy of Europe. Sumptuary laws, designed to ensure that the general population was dressed according to their station, issued strict edicts related to mourning attire until the end of the sixteenth century.[3] These regulations, along with the high price of black dye, meant that mourning apparel was rarely worn by the working classes.

But as the Industrial Revolution increased the buying power of the middle class and manufacturing allowed for the mass production of black fabrics and crape, mourning dress proliferated throughout every level of society. Wearing proper mourning attire actually became a sign of respectability, especially during the Victorian era, and was a way for the lower classes to assert their socioeconomic mobility.[4] Sorrow had suddenly become chic.

Undertakers and the fashion industry alike benefited from the popularization of grief etiquette during that era. The commercialization of mourning clothes corresponded with the widespread publication and consumption of fashion magazines and home journals. These magazines spelled out with arduous specificity the expectations and protocols around mourning dress, though the details would vary from publication to publication.[5] Social pitfalls abounded, and navigating this complex maze of proprieties added an entirely new level of stress and expense for the already bereft mourner, eager to honor the dead and also eager to prove their own reputability.

Clothing customs were most consequential for women. By the mid-nineteenth century, men could get away with simply wearing a black suit and tie, along with a black armband or hatband. Women, however, did not get off so easily. Historian Lou Taylor writes, "Women were used, albeit willingly and even eagerly by most, as a show piece, to display their family's total respectability, sense of conformity, and wealth."[6] There were all kinds of rules about fabrics, trim, collars, and colors.

Different publications recommended various mourning time frames for different family relations, with each stage of mourning requiring different accessories, fabrics, and shades of muted colors. Generally speaking, the recommendation was that children should mourn for parents—and parents should mourn for children—one year. For grandparents and siblings, the mourning period was six months. For aunts and uncles, two months was required; for cousins, four weeks.[7]

Pressure was perhaps greatest for a Victorian widow. Her period of mourning lasted two and a half years. During the first year of deep mourning, she was required to live in seclusion, leaving her home only to attend church and see close relatives. She was to wear only black, preferably wool fabric with collars and cuffs of folded, untrimmed black crape. The following year, she entered "second mourning" and was allowed to lose some of the crape, add some silk, wear black lace at the dress cuffs and collar, and expand her social circle. In the last half year, known as "half-mourning," she was permitted to wear clothing that was white, gray, and mauve.[8]

Mourning dress became a regular part of the average Victorian woman's wardrobe. With mortality rates as high as they were, it wasn't unusual for a person to spend a large portion of life in mourning clothes. Ladies had to find creative ways to make their grief glamorous. Memento mori jewelry was highly fashionable; necklaces, rings, and brooches bearing an image of the lost loved one, a skull and crossbones, or designs woven with hair of the deceased were very popular. There were plenty of other accessories to complete the look: bonnets, gloves, fans, and black-bordered handkerchiefs.

The crape veil was particularly important for the ensemble. In the first year of mourning for a widow, the veil was to be long, thick, and made of crape. During the second year of mourning, the veil could be shortened and made of tulle or net.[9] Met museum curator Jessica Regan notes, "The mourning veil was often described as a means of shielding the mourner and hiding her grief." This protective aspect of mourning clothes was not the only function. Regan says, "Mourning dress was also a form of public display, viewed by some women as an outer expression of inner feelings."[10]

Unfortunately, the iconic veil did not come without its hazards. Mourning crape, usually made of silk, wool, or a combination of both, was stiff, flaky, easily snagged, foul-smelling, and saturated with toxic chemicals. The fabric would bleed easily in rain and humidity or if met with the tears or sweat of the wearer. The dark stains on the skin of the widow were not easily removed by soap and water. The problem was so prevalent that popular ladies' magazines would feature articles on how to remove the stains with various concoctions of cream of tartar and oxalic acid. Physicians from that era warned of the health risks associated with the wearing of crape veils.[11] But that did little to dissuade mourners from meeting the societal expectations of the day.

Bizarrely, this perilous black veil also came to be somewhat of a sex symbol. The young, mourning widow was often seen as incredibly enticing, free of her marital commitment, vulnerable, yet alluringly untouchable. She was the epitome of elegant mystique beneath her darkened shroud.[12]

The traditions of grief are only as pure as the people practicing them. No grief ritual is perfect. The bereavement etiquette of the Victorian era is proof of that. Any ritual is susceptible to becoming rote or performative. Plenty of rituals have been manipulated or hijacked by profiteers to plunder the weak and make a show of social or religious superiority. It's easy to take advantage of an opportunity as recurrent and universal as death.

Perhaps Queen Victoria herself, the century's most exemplary griever, modeled most powerfully what it means to truly and authentically *wear mourning*. The "Widow of Windsor," as she was called, was undeterred by the criticism of her subjects who questioned her sanity and longed for the days of frivolity to return to court. She persisted in her overt and obtrusive bereavement rituals, wearing black until the day she died, never fully emerging from her life of seclusion. By all accounts, this was not a matter of show or a strict adherence to social propriety. She was truly heartbroken. If she was trying to impress anyone, she had failed. Some thought she had gone mad.

The queen seemed to understand something many of us forget today. She recognized the wily, elongated nature of bereavement—that there's no timeline for grief; that it cannot be contained by mere codes of conduct; that there's nothing decorous whatsoever about grief.

• • • • •

The imagery of ocean waves has long been used to describe grief, so I guess I knew to expect surges of sadness to ebb and flow, for the intensity to rise and fall depending on the hour or the day.

But grief is not simply sadness. This is something I wish I'd known beforehand. I was under the impression that the emotion of grief was straightforward. When a person died, you would feel very sad to lose them. In my mind, grief was heart-wrenching, of course, but clean-cut and square-shooting.

I never expected the noise of grief, the frenzy of emotions that ensued. I tried in vain to keep it all hidden. The surface was a tightly controlled veneer, thin and taut. Underneath, everything was chaotic, swirling, and turbulent. I was experiencing all kinds of feelings. Confusion (what exactly had just happened?); fear (life will never feel safe again); anger (why did God let this happen?); dread (everyone I've ever loved will die); guilt (why did she die and I get to go on living?). Strangest of all, I felt a deep sense of shame and embarrassment. How could I ever have been so foolish? What made me think I would always be happy?

No one ever told me that grief also forces you to bear witness to the pain of the people you love most in the world. You watch your family walk through the worst experience of their lives. It is absolutely gutting to see your parents lose their child, your niece and nephew lose a mother, or your husband lose a baby. It can be hard to differentiate between your emotions and theirs, to know how to shoulder their burdens while staggering under your own. We all lost the same person. But we lost her in different ways, and we all grieved her differently.

Sadness? I didn't have space in my brain for it. Frankly, simple sadness would have felt like a luxury. Grief wasn't a wave. It was a hurricane!

I am glad that society no longer asks us to hide our emotions. Somewhere along the way in the last twenty years, culture has given us permission to be honest, at least in part. We can say when we are hurting, ask for help when we are lost. Most of my friends who are my age meet regularly with a therapist and we congratulate ourselves publicly for doing so.

But there are some rules of decorum that endure. Threads of toxic positivity weave their persistent way through our narratives. We can admit that we are struggling, but we'd better resolve the conversation with a clear articulation of our hope. We can state that we need help, but we'd better be careful not to scare people.

As I've said before, it's uncomfortable being the elephant in the room. I went to a baby shower shortly after my sister died and I remember feeling so awkward, like I'd brought some dark cloud of sadness into the room. On my drive to the event, I rehearsed a few talking points—a positive, hopeful framing of the way I was feeling. Then, I crossed my fingers and prayed that no one would approach me with that concerned face, the furrowed brow and pursed lips, and ask how I was *really* doing.

Somehow, though, I was also simultaneously *afraid* that no one would ask! I was scared that my pain was invisible, that I was forgotten. These conflicting desires, these inexplicable emotions—this is why the bereaved so often just want to stay home and hide.

Sometimes it's hard to describe what's going on inside my heart to my closest *friends*, much less to strangers and the general public that I interact with every day. The incoherence of bereavement isn't exactly the kind of thing that can be articulated in a succinct sound bite. There's no elevator speech for grief.

How do you concisely explain to the grocery attendant, the hairdresser, the barista, the dentist, the doctor, or the auto mechanic that you are simply not yourself because you've lost someone? Yes, I left my wallet in the car. No, I haven't been using conditioner. Yes, I'm crying into my coffee mug. No, I haven't been flossing regularly.

Yes, I think I'm going to die from this common cold. No, I didn't notice the squealing sound my brakes were making. Because I'm in grief. Because my mind is moving in a million different directions. Because I lost my baby. Because my sister died after being hospitalized for "just the flu." Because today is her birthday. Because today is the anniversary of my miscarriage. Because this office smells like the antiseptic we used to clean mortar wounds. Because I've been debilitated in a million different ways, and I know the growth and redemption and wisdom are coming but they're not here yet. They're just not.

Before the Industrial Revolution, "living locally" was the only way to live. The world was primarily agrarian and people's lives were situated entirely within close-knit towns and villages. Families were thoroughly integrated into small communities made up of neighbors and relatives who would have known if you had been sick, had a baby, or lost a loved one. Understanding was automatic; grace was a given. But today, our lives are lost in crowded urban populations. We don't personally know the butcher, the baker, or the candlestick maker. Most of the people we pass on the street don't know us from Adam. We are storyless scenery in one another's lives.

I remember so many times feeling all alone, standing there in my street clothes, surrounded by strangers who had no idea what I was going through. Maybe if I'd been like a Victorian woman, decked out in the regalia of grief—a black dress or a long dark veil—people would have been moved to forbearance before interacting with me. Maybe I wouldn't have been cut off in traffic. Maybe people would have let me move to the front of the line at the grocery store. Someone might have paid for my coffee. Someone would have held the door for me; maybe given me the best parking space. This public, communal kindness would not have solved the problem or brought an end to my bereavement. But it would have been a comfort. It would have made me feel safe to be broken.

In spite of grief, the days trudge on. Diapers need changing; groceries need buying. We stumble into work, into church. We host dinner parties and show up to business meetings. Life marches steadily forward and our grief just gets dragged along. No one wants to dolefully remind people of their own inadequacy. "Just a quick refresher, folks: remember that I'm not quite at the top of my game yet, seeing as how my sister is still dead and all." Meghan O'Rourke writes, "Without ritual, the only way to share a loss was to talk about it…I wanted a way to show my grief rather than tell it."[13]

• • • • •

It's difficult to know the true function of mourning clothes. Certainly, the Victorian era was fraught with truly unhelpful protocols and formalities. Yet, similar to a wedding, with all its pomp and circumstance and fretting over clothing, the dress codes of mourning were a way of marking that a significant life change had occurred, that things would never be the same again. Perhaps, as many claimed, all the p's and q's were so rigidly upheld simply from a desire to truly honor the dead, to make much ado about their lives and their passings.

Maybe for women, particularly widows, it was a way to creatively express their own individuality in the midst of grief. The memento mori jewelry, the various and inventive uses of crape, the fashionable black dresses—perhaps it was all a way of saying, "*I'm still here*, even though my loved one is not."

It's possible that it was all simply a socio-economic exhibition, a way of "keeping up with the Joneses" and proving your fiscal respectability. Maybe mourning dress protocols were an assertion of dignity in the face of death. Or maybe fussing over the accessories of sorrow was a nerve-racking but much-needed distraction.

It was perhaps the Great War that nudged Europe away from its strict, performative dress codes of grief. As casualties mounted, grieving women were too busy with the war effort back home to retreat into seclusion and fuss about the painstaking details of clothing. Many believe it was an issue of morale, that to see the streets flooded with droves of women shrouded in black crape would have been unbearable, both for the soldiers home on leave and for the public in general.

These days, most of the Western world has all but lost the uniform of bereavement. Other cultures around the world have maintained the rituals of mourning dress. My friend Sophea tells me that in her home country of Cambodia, people are still expected to wear white if a loved one dies. White is the color of mourning in many Asian cultures and is a symbol of purity and rebirth. Red is worn by grieving families in parts of Africa, particularly South Africa, where the color is associated with the devastating losses of apartheid. Other physical manifestations of grief exist around the world. In some Hindu cultures it is customary to shave your head when a family member dies. Sophea tells me this is common in Cambodia as well. Up until recently, the women of the Dani tribe of Papua New Guinea would amputate the tips of their fingers when a loved one passed, in part to placate the departed but also as a physical manifestation of their loss.[14]

Of all the rituals I've studied, wearing black is perhaps the one I most wish we could bring back. I like to think that at its core, mourning dress is simply an outward expression of internal sorrow, a way of marking yourself as bereft so that the world will know there is a deep ache inside of you. "I don't wear black because it becomes me...I wear mourning because it corresponds with my feelings," wrote teenager Nannie Haskins of Tennessee, who lost her brother in the Civil War. After being told that black was becoming on her she responded, "Becomes me fiddlestick. What do I care whether it becomes me or *not*?"[15]

• • • • •

I am a very private person. I'm a fairly extreme introvert, in fact. The thought of inviting people into any part of my story of grief feels a little overwhelming. There will always be aspects of my experience that belong only to me and to my family. They are details too personal and painful to share. But even opening the door just a little feels pretty scary sometimes.

Regardless of the fear, I believe wholeheartedly in the power of shared story. We need the guidance and wisdom gained by others who have gone before us on the journey of grief. We need solidarity, to feel like we are not alone, and we are not crazy. It was that conviction that led me to explore historic rituals of grief in the first place.

But I've tried hard to walk the line between vulnerability and exhibitionism. I'm glad that society no longer requires us to put on a brave face and suffer alone in silence. But in a world that (rightly) affirms the pain of our individual experiences, we can sometimes (wrongly) wear our trauma like a badge of honor, or like a curio that makes us interesting or credible.

Our culture has almost commodified candor, with social media accounts and podcasts dedicated to the managed exhibition of our deepest sorrows and frustrations. Authenticity is a currency and entire industries are built on finding creative ways to make our failures flattering. Leave it to capitalism, I guess, to assign commercial value to something as sacred and mysterious as bereavement.

I realize the irony of my critique when I have, in fact, chosen to write a book about grief.

It's worth asking why we, like the Victorians, feel this draw toward performance in the midst of loss. Maybe this is it: Death humiliated me. It was mortifying. Sometimes I think I'm trying to win back my dignity, my self-respect. I'm trying to remind myself and the world that *I'm still here*, because there were times when I almost wasn't.

The truth is, I want it both ways. I want people to notice my pain, but not in a voyeuristic way. I want people's support, but not their speculation. I want to be seen without having to showboat. But I'm smart enough to know we live in such a noisy world that sometimes we have to wave our arms to be noticed.

Meghan O'Rourke writes about "the difference between being and seeming, the uncertainty about how the inner translates into the outer, the sense that one is expected to perform grief palatably. (If you don't seem sad, people worry; but if you are grief-stricken, people flinch away from your pain.)"[16] And if I am silent, I worry sometimes that no one sees me at all.

O'Rourke articulates something I feel deep in my bones. Despite my inherent millennial propensity toward performance, I, like everyone else in the world, want to be loved without having to put on an act, to be seen without having to put on a show. As Jan Richardson says, "So many of us carry griefs that we don't feel like we can speak. But there is something about grief that wants to be seen. There's something about grief that wants to be known."[17]

• • • • •

The mourning dress of the Old Testament and much of the ancient world was sackcloth. Scholars believe sackcloth was likely dark in color and made of goat's or camel's hair. The material could be used for making tents, sails, or carpet, but throughout the ancient Near East, in times of repentance and grief, it was worn as clothing. The fabric was coarse and often placed directly on the skin, which was no doubt uncomfortable.[18] It was worn full-length, with a tie at the waist, or as a plain loincloth.[19] Many times, sackcloth was accompanied by ashes, which were a mark of death and destruction, a physical representation of human mortality before God.[20]

I was talking with my friend Ethan about this and he commented that most of us in modern-day America would likely choose to put on our comfort clothes—sweatpants, T-shirt, cozy socks—to work through the ravages of bereavement. Sackcloth, in contrast, was rough against the body, a physical embodiment of the nettling discomfort of grief. I am reminded of what seems to be true about many ancient rituals. They are not inherently placating. They almost seemed designed to rub salt in the wound, to guide you deeper and deeper into the dark hole of grief. What is tangible and visible matches what is going on inside. These embodied genuflections of grief correspond with our internal pain.

We see examples of sackcloth being worn throughout the Bible. Jacob tore his clothes and put on sackcloth when he thought his son Joseph had been killed by a ferocious animal (see Gen. 37:34). When the child he had with Bathsheba was ill, King David fasted and wore sackcloth for seven days, pleading with God to spare his son's life (see 2 Sam. 12:16). When Mordecai learned of the edict to destroy the Jews, he tore his clothes, put on sackcloth, and went into the city wailing (see Est. 4:1). The king of Ninevah, when confronted with his sin before God, commanded that all the people and even the livestock cover themselves in sackcloth as a sign of repentance (see Jon. 3:6–8).

In the Old Testament, the rituals of grief mirror the rituals of repentance. In fact, most passages that reference sackcloth are stories of remorse, the people of God responding with conviction over their sins. In light of this, I've asked myself what repentance and grief have in common. If nothing else, both bereavement and contrition bring you to the end of yourself. Sin and sorrow are humiliating. They reveal how weak you are in your own flesh. Both require us to turn in a different direction, to abandon our own plans and move toward God.

Wailing. Ashes. Sackcloth. All are outward expressions of spiritual catastrophe. We are ruined and there is no shame in showing it to the world.

Job, as archetypal in his grief as Queen Victoria, was very familiar with sackcloth and ashes. He makes a poignant statement in Job 16:15. In the verse just prior, Job is railing against his friends for offering him long-winded speeches instead of comfort. He laments that God seems to have attacked him. He then says that he had "sewed sackcloth over [his] skin." It is evocative imagery, recognizing the visceral and enduring nature of his grief. Nowhere else in Scripture does someone speak so corporeally and permanently of sackcloth. In this moment, Job sees no way out of his sorrow. He will wear the garb of grief forever.

The timeline for the wearing of mourning clothes may vary by era and culture. But those of us who have lost someone we deeply love know that there is no end date or grand finale to grief. How do we persevere through the long, humiliating journey of loss? Do we hide forever beneath our thickening skin, ashamed to show the world the pain we are enduring in our hearts? Do we admit the defeat of it all? Do we show our scars?

Miraculously, God has given us an example of enduring sorrow. Jesus Himself wears the scars of His grief *forever*. Love led Him to the trauma of death, nails in the hands and feet and a spear through the side. Even when He returned triumphantly in His resurrected body, He felt no need to erase the visible signs of His suffering. The atoning climax of the cross, His passion for the world, and His sorrow for its suffering were nothing to hide or be ashamed of. Once again, God made a display of His vulnerability. Incarnate love. Incarnate grief. His wounds remained and will remain for eternity.

What a remarkable choice on the part of God, to acknowledge that candor and honesty don't diminish the courage or victory. God was not embarrassed by the humiliation of death: "This is my body, which is for you" (1 Cor. 11:24). It is through brokenness that we are made whole. This is the path of pain and joy. This visibly wounded presence is the way God chose to show up in His glory.

If Jesus wore the scars of His sorrow and sacrifice into the resurrection, perhaps we will too. In the life to come, I'm guessing we'll all have moved past the desire to perform or pretend. If it's attention we are seeking, it will be to a different end. I think we'll be communally reveling in the shared joy of having overcome, of persevering. Maybe then we will all look death in the eye and point proudly to our battle marks. With the same triumph of Christ, we will say, "Hey, Death, look what you did! But guess what? You *did not win*."

CHAPTER 9

TOLLING THE BELL

(ENDURANCE)

Love never fails.

—1 Corinthians 13:8

In the Middle Ages, it was not uncommon to hear the clang of a bell resounding across the countryside as the ominous clouds of a thunderstorm rolled in. That was because people once believed that evil spirits were present in the tempest, and that the sound of a church bell was powerful enough to cause those evil spirits to flee.

In those days, church bells were named, blessed, baptized, and commissioned for service in the spiritual warfare that was waged in the air all around. It was thought that there was a supernatural force in the toll of a bell. The inscriptions etched on the bells told the story of their powers: "Fulmina Frango" (I break the lightning); "Fulgura Compello" (I drive away the thunder); "Cunctorum Vox Daemoniorum" (My voice is the slayer of demons); "Pestem Fugo" (I put the plague to flight).[1]

Because of this belief, it was also customary to ring a bell when someone in the community was on their deathbed or in extremis. This was known as the *passing bell* and to ring it was a tactic of offense against the evil spiritual forces that were thought to be particularly active at the point of death. It was also a call for the community to pray. If demons and devils were making a special effort to obtain possession of the soul of the sick, then a resounding bell and the intercessions of God's people were a holy force to be reckoned with.

Thirteenth-century canonist William Durandus wrote about the deep sense of confidence that society had in their communal bells: "That by their sound the faithful may be mutually cheered on towards their reward; that the devotion of faith may be increased in them; that their fruits of the field, their minds and their bodies may be defended; that the hostile legions and all the snares of the Enemy may be repulsed; that the rattling hail, the whirlwinds, and the violence of tempests and lightning may be restrained."[2]

In his famous *Devotions Upon Emergent Occasions*, John Donne, who was convalescing after a life-threatening illness, tells us that the passing bell, no matter whose illness it is proclaiming, serves as a reminder to the whole community that every one of us is ephemeral. Because mortality is a universal human condition, we are all one. We share in one another's sorrow and in one another's mortality. "Therefore," he writes, "never send to know for whom the bell tolls; it tolls for thee."

In extremis—to be at the extremity, at the point of death. An invalid, an old man, a woman in labor, a child weakened by disease. As they lay in their beds and teetered on the edge of eternity, the people of God prayed. While the passing bell may have waged war against the dark forces of the air, more often than not death still seized its victim. The commotion and tumult of the illness, the raging battle against mortality, would come to a crashing halt. Life on this earth was over.

But there is another bell for that moment.

• • • • •

Closure. Letting go. Resolved grief. Filling the void.

These are concepts I've never been able to really get onboard with. The fact is that years after my losses, I still don't feel like I've come to a clear sense of redemption. That's not to say I think I'm suffering from what some psychologists have called "chronic grief" or "prolonged grief disorder."[3] I'm no longer in shock, and the grief doesn't typically impede my ability to function on any given day. But I still feel deeply and profoundly wounded by it all.

I was told that if I viewed my loved one's dead body, that if I attended the funeral, that if I went through her things, it would help with the closure. Perhaps those rituals aided in my acceptance of what occurred. I suppose that's no small thing. But closure to me indicates a cessation. Resolution implies that the dissonance of death has somehow harmonized, as if mortality made some sort of peace offering and now we are once again on friendly terms. Letting go feels like I somehow close the loop, that I bid grief farewell and move steadily along as if nothing has happened.

But all grief is chronic to some degree. Nothing fills the void of the person you lost. Contrary to popular belief, having a baby does not mentally and emotionally undo a previous miscarriage. Making new friends does not lessen the pain of losing a friend. Remarrying does not replace the deceased spouse. There is no "recovery" from that kind of pain.

It seems to me like grief has taken up permanent residence in my life, like a bad roommate who always leaves a mess, clutters up my well-ordered existence, and never pays her share of the rent. There's no way to evict grief, nowhere for grief to go. It's a parasite, a freeloader, a leech.

• • • • •

While the passing bell was rung as a herald of death, a different toll-ing, known as the death knell, was sounded immediately after the individual actually passed away. One purpose of the death knell was to communicate to the community *who* had passed away. In fact, the word "toll" is derived from the word "tell," as bells were said to provide notification or "be tellers" of the news of death.

Different regions had various systems worked out for commu-nicating the specifics, but generally speaking it was common for two strikes—or two "tells"—of the bell to indicate a woman had died, and three "tells" if a man had died. Tones of the bell had meaning too. Tenor bells were rung for adults and treble bells were rung for children. After a pause, it was customary to announce the age of the deceased with one stroke for every year corresponding to their age. Denoting the gender as well as the age was how people would know who had died.[4]

To set the sound apart from the ring of a typical church bell, a bell used for a death knell would be half-muffled. Part of the bell's clapper would be covered with a leather muffler, which produced a softer chime.[5] Bells were later tolled again at the funeral and burial of the deceased.

A bell was certainly not the only instrument used throughout history and culture to announce a death. The African tradition of beating the "drum of death" continued to be practiced on some plantations in the American South when a slave died. The sound of the drum of death informed the community of the loss and summoned mourners.[6] Brass instruments were sometimes played at a church to announce a death, and we are all familiar with the mournful sound of taps being played to honor fallen military servicemembers.

The use of the death knell as a means of communication persisted well into the 1900s in Appalachia because telephones and other modern means of communication were so scarce in the mountains. One individual testified to the use of the death knell in Cades Cove, Tennessee:

> You can feel the silence pass over the community as all activity is stopped and the number of rings is counted. One, two, three—it must be the Myer's baby that has the fever. No, it's still tolling—four, five, six. There is another pause at twenty—could that be Molly Shields? Her baby is due at any time now—no, it's still tolling. Will it never stop? Thirty-eight, thirty-nine, another pause—who? It couldn't be Ben; he was here just yesterday; said he was feeling fit as a fiddle—no, it's starting again. Seventy, seventy-one, seventy-two. Silence. You listen, but there is no sound— only silence. Isaac Tipton. He has been ailing for two weeks now. It must be Isaac.[7]

Somewhere along the way, the death knell ceased to be a commonly practiced ritual, but the memory of it continued on through the ages as a well-known idiom in the English language. We now use it to note the end of an endeavor, to indicate something has met its doom. Some even mix and match their idioms and refer to a death *nail*, when really what they are probably getting at is a "nail in the coffin." Same difference, I guess.

The death knell is cessation. It is the end. With it comes finality.

In one sense, death always happens abruptly. It is a clear moment, a before and after. Even if the illness is long and drawn out, the passing itself happens in the blink of an eye. One moment a person has breath, a beating heart, some sign of life, feeble though it may be. And then, suddenly, they don't. Capacity for consciousness and brain stem function is lost. They flatline, expire, and pass into the unknown of the afterlife.

The finality of death stands in stark contrast to the ongoing nature of grief. Contrary to what the idiom would have us believe, a death knell was actually intentionally long and drawn out, a measured, plodding toll. It went on and on. The word "knell" is derived from the Old English word "cnyll," which means "a sound made by a bell when struck or rung slowly."[8] The death knell is sustained, spacious enough for contemplation, for dread. It is haunting.

What is true of the ritual is true in life: Death is fast. But grief is slow.

• • • • •

In 1969, Elisabeth Kübler-Ross introduced her famous Five Stages of Grief in her book *On Death and Dying*. Though critics have long questioned the validity of Kübler-Ross's approach, citing a lack of empirical research, the Five Stages (Denial, Anger, Bargaining, Depression, and Acceptance) have become ingrained in our subconscious. They've provided a lexicon with which we talk about the complexity of the various emotions surrounding bereavement.

Even Kübler-Ross herself, in her final book, *On Grief and Grieving*, which she cowrote with David Kessler, noted that grief is much more complex than a simple understanding of the stages suggests. "They were never meant to help tuck messy emotions into neat packages...There is not a typical response to loss, as there is no typical loss. Our grief is as individual as our lives. Not everyone goes through all of [the stages] or goes in a prescribed order."[9]

The Five Stages is a woefully inadequate model and yet, despite its critics, the model may forever be a part of our vernacular when we speak about grief. Perhaps we are lured by the false hope that we might be able to categorize the journey of bereavement into five tidy stages that one can move through linearly and consecutively. It's enticing to think we can methodically progress from stage to stage, acquiring mastery over one before we advance on to the next, ticking boxes as we go. Eventually all the boxes are ticked, and we graduate from grief.

But grief has a way of defying our most well-constructed strictures. Proverb 30:15–16 articulates the enduring tenacity of grief: "There are three things that are never satisfied, four that never say, 'Enough!'; the grave, the barren womb, land, which is never satisfied with water, and fire, which never says, 'Enough!'" Death never seems to be satisfied. Grief doesn't give up. It persists. You never graduate from grief.

Even when the initial anguish of grief has abated, all kinds of random occurrences can trigger a surge of sorrow: filling out family medical history paperwork; opening a kitchen drawer and seeing the napkin holders my grandmother gave me; cleaning the bathroom, where the smell of bleach takes me back to a hospital room; hearing a song come on the radio that I listened to while in a war zone; chatting with a new acquaintance who asks a simple question: "Do you have any siblings?" or "How many children do you have?" Learning to live with grief is learning how to navigate a million mundane, tiny, brutal reminders of what you've lost.

As we have seen, different cultures have acknowledged the duration of grief in their rituals. The Victorians believed that a widow should grieve two and a half years. My Iraqi friend Sargon shared with me that where he was brought up, if a close family member died, you were expected to grieve for a year, and to refrain from parties or wedding celebrations. In Jewish culture, a child grieves a parent for an additional eleven months—known as *shnat ha-evel*—after the first month of mourning. These timelines typically allow more space than the American norm of expecting someone to bounce back a few weeks after a loss. But even the most generous expectations fall short in acknowledging the lifelong nature of grief.

Six months after my sister's death, when Tim and I were renovating our bathroom, we went to Lowe's hardware store to pick out some accessories. I suddenly found myself weeping while looking at the toilet paper holders. Growing up, Rachel and I shared a bathroom, and we had one of those old-school chrome spring-loaded toilet paper holders. It was tedious to change and would shoot back in your face if you didn't handle it properly. That device may have been the greatest source of our childhood conflicts. Neither of us liked to change it out, and we each would frequently leave empty tubes on the holder, hoping the other would deal with it. Seeing the simplicity of the dispensers they now had on display would have made Rachel laugh as we reminisced about our passionate sisterly rows.

How do you explain to the Lowe's associate why you are crying in the bathroom accessories aisle? At funerals and memorial services, we are prepared to lose our composure. But how can you steel yourself or explain yourself when grief sneaks up in the most unsuspecting and inconvenient moments?

Meghan O'Rourke writes, "My mother's death was not a single event, but a whole series of events—the first Easter without her; the first wedding anniversary without her…The lesson lay in the empty chair at the dinner table. It was learned night after night, day after day. And so you always feel suspense, a queer dread—you never know what occasion will break the loss freshly open."[10]

These moments don't go away. They keep happening. Just when you think you've moved past stage five, you are startled to find yourself tumbling back into stage one. You have not moved on; you have not healed. Yes, the shock may have worn off. The adrenaline surge of trying to survive may have subsided. But now you are on the grief hamster wheel. Now it's just the steady hum of sadness that she is still, still, still gone.

• • • • •

The passing bells, death knells, and funeral bells fell out of common use for a variety of reasons. As urban centers became more densely populated, bells lost their effectiveness as a tool of communication. Neighbors didn't know neighbors, so it became increasingly difficult to know for whom the bell actually tolled. Newspapers and telephones became more effective ways of informing friends and loved ones about deaths. And of course, now we have Facebook.

As we saw in the case of the Black Plague and the Great War, widespread catastrophic events impacted the use of rituals, this time, bell ringing. Significant smallpox and yellow fever outbreaks in the United States in the late 1700s led to ordinances limiting the tolling of bells. It was thought that the continuous, ominous sound of death knells and funeral bells would afflict the living with fear and weaken with dread those who were already sick with the disease. In 1793, publisher Mathew Carey wrote that in Philadelphia the funeral bells had "been kept pretty constantly going the whole day, so as to terrify those in health, and drive the sick, as far as the influence of imagination could produce that effect, to their graves."[11] Some rituals, even though they are meant to honor and aid in closure, can be demoralizing.

Two centuries earlier, the death knell and the excessive use of funeral bells were suppressed by the Reformers because they felt that ringing bells for the dead could too easily be construed as an invitation to pray for departed souls in purgatory, a thoroughly Catholic practice.[12] As I've learned is often the case, the church has a tendency to stamp out rituals they find are rooted in bad theology. I can understand this to some degree. But there's an important theological truth beneath the ritual of the bells that I'm afraid was also lost.

Our ancestors acknowledged the spiritual battle that rages all around us, particularly in times of death. It was a fear of demons that led them to "conceal" themselves in black clothing and avoid staring into the mirror for too long. They would ring bells to counteract the evil spirits that hovered around a deathbed. Our forebears had a respect for the reality of spiritual warfare and took ritualistic measures to engage in it. I understand that the tactics they employed may have seemed more like pagan superstitions to some, and I know the Reformers were eager to put an end to Catholic customs they viewed as misguided. But I'm afraid in our efforts to regulate this ritual, we've forgotten how susceptible we are to malevolent powers when we are in grief.

I still believe that the ruler of this age prowls around like a lion looking for someone to devour. The mourner is the perfect prey, their faith upended, their sense of security shattered. When love is bereft of the object of its affection, it can easily wander off into the void. The Enemy's tactic is total warfare. Nothing is off-limits or untouched.

Bells wage war. Rituals wage war. They name the enemy and chart a strategy to outflank, attack, and subdue. But bells, like so many other rituals, have been decommissioned, discharged from service. "My voice is the slayer of demons." My apologies to John Donne, but I can't help but wonder for whom the bell tolls *now*. Anyone at all?

• • • • •

Nicholas Wolterstorff writes about the loss of his son to a climbing accident in his book *Lament for a Son*. He began writing in the immediate aftermath of the loss, but later he reflected on how his grief changed over time: "Rather often I am asked whether the grief remains as intense as when I wrote. The answer is, No. The wound is no longer raw. But it has not disappeared. That is as it should be. If he was worth loving, he is worth grieving over. Grief is an existential testimony to the worth of the one loved. That worth abides."[13] I suppose it's the difference between moving on *from* versus moving forward *with*. Wherever I go, my grief goes with me.

Love is a powerful thing. First Corinthians 13 tells us a lot about what love should look like. It's patient. It's kind. It doesn't envy or boast. It's not proud and it doesn't dishonor others. It's not self-seeking or easily angered. It doesn't keep a record of wrongs or delight in evil. It rejoices in the truth and protects. It trusts. It hopes.

But what does love look like when the object of the love no longer exists, at least not physically in time and space? Is love just a memory? Is it past tense? Is it delusional to love someone who is gone? Plenty of people have reflected on the fact that grief is not the absence of love. Rather, it is simply love reborn, remade into something new.

Paul's conclusion on the matter of love is what impresses me the most. He says that it "always perseveres" (1 Cor. 13:7). The Greek word Paul uses here is *hypomenei*, which means "to remain under." He finishes his exposition by saying that "love never fails" (13:8).

Love never fails. That has always been a fairly intimidating statement to me, as if Paul expected real love to always be perfect, to never make a mistake. But Greek scholars have noted that the common translation here is somewhat inadequate. They believe that the phrase is more accurately understood as "Love never comes to an end." It should communicate the idea that love never disappears or diminishes. It will never cease to be. It will never become invalid or obsolete.[14]

Dietrich Bonhoeffer writes:

There is nothing that can replace the absence of someone dear to us, and one should not even attempt to do so. One must simply hold out and endure it. At first that sounds very hard, but at the same time it is also a great comfort. For to the extent the emptiness truly remains unfilled one remains connected to the other person through it. It is wrong to say that God fills the emptiness. God in no way fills it but much more leaves it precisely unfilled and thus helps us preserve—even in pain—the authentic relationship. Furthermore, the more beautiful and full the remembrances, the more difficult the separation. But gratitude transforms the torment of memory into silent joy. One bears what was lovely in the past not as a thorn but as a precious gift deep within, a hidden treasure of which one can always be certain.[15]

What does it mean to grieve? I've heard the word, said the word, and written the word a million times and yet as I type this, it occurs to me that I'm not entirely sure what it means. Is to grieve to feel sad? To miss someone? Is it reorganizing your world around a massive hole?

And what exactly is the work of grief? Freud was the first to introduce the concept of "grief work." It was his belief that hypothetical psychic energy was bound up with the memory of the deceased. Grief work, in his estimation, was when little by little, memory by memory, the bereaved released their attachment to the deceased and set free the energy that was bound up with them.[16]

As much as I've read about this, I'll admit my understanding falls a bit short. To me, the work of grief is less about release and more about learning how to *hold on* in a way that is healthy and whole. To grieve is to love. The labor of love, in the face of unspeakable loss, *is* the grief work. Meghan O'Rourke notes that the word "grief" is derived from an old French word meaning "to burden."[17] Grief is learning to endure, to bear up under the beautiful burden of love.

Hypomenei, "to persevere," is the same Greek root word James uses when talking about perseverance (*hypomone*) in the first chapter of his epistle: "You know that the testing of your faith produces perseverance. Let perseverance finish its work so that you may be mature and complete, not lacking anything" (1:3–4). The word literally means "to remain under." It means "to stay." To carry. To grieve is to endure. To grieve is to remain.

My friend Bev is especially passionate about this Greek word *hypomone*. After twenty-two years of working in the aid world, responding to hurricanes, wars, and epidemics, she knows a thing or two about bearing up under a heavy load. She tells me she first learned the concept of endurance as a kid growing up in the Yukon of Canada, a wild and frozen landscape where it wasn't uncommon to have bears as neighbors. When I ask her what perseverance means to her, she tells me she pictures a traveler far from home, pressing into the cold Yukon wind as the sun sets. "Perseverance is staying on the trail," she says, trusting that it will lead you where you need to go. Perseverance is leaning into the elements. She says it's unwavering and consistent, never swerving from its purpose.

Hypomone is not passive, as a term like "patience" might indicate. Rather, *hypomone* is an active noun. We always laugh that Bev is the best teammate to send into a disaster zone first, because when you give her a mission, she is like a dog after a bone. She leans into the elements and carries the purpose forward.

This disposition of hers came in especially handy when she was diagnosed with stage four cancer last year. When it came to confronting the challenge of cancer, Bev was a dog after a bone. She bore up under the burden of treatment and illness with tenacity and strength. She committed to the path of healing, physically, mentally, and emotionally. She didn't run away or try to bypass the pain.

She stayed in the game. She remained fully present in the journey every single day, and still does.

Bev was one of a small number of heroic people who fought on the front lines of the Ebola outbreak in Liberia. As a water and sanitation technician, she worked in a treatment unit and saw firsthand what Ebola does to its victims. She told me that at one time, when the unit was bursting at the seams with patients who were experiencing the most violent stages of the disease, she had a moment where she completely froze. She said it was like all the sound dropped out of the room as the chaos swirled around her. She remembered that she could almost see the spiritual forces of good and evil swirling frantically above her, the demons summoned at the imminence of death, the angels rallying for a counterattack.

Love kept Bev's feet grounded when she could have fled, when she could have hopped on a plane and gone home. Love "puts the plague to flight." Love is the "slayer of demons." Love endures. Love remains behind when everyone else leaves. Love stays on the path. Love carries. Love never fails.

●　●　●　●　●

Sometimes, the thing you thought would kill you...doesn't. So you go on living as the walking wounded.

"But, Amanda, how are you doing...*really*?"

It's a question I've come to dread because the answer is so complex. People will never be satisfied with the response "I'm okay!" They'll assume I'm avoiding the question or hiding my struggle. They are trying to show they care, trying to probe in order to support.

But sometimes the answer "I'm okay" is genuine. Because I *am* okay. And also, I am *not okay*. Herein lies the concept I've struggled most to articulate as I write and talk about grief: how you can be two things at once; how you can be both *not okay* and *okay* at the same time; how you can be simultaneously broken but strangely mended. I do not have closure. I have not resolved anything. Redemption has not presented itself to me in a neat, tidy box. I have not passed through all the stages. I have not graduated from grief. I did not earn an A+.

And also, I am breathing. I am surviving. I have not given up.

In his book *The Other Side of Sadness*, psychologist George A. Bonanno challenges conventional views of the grief process, including Kübler-Ross's five stages and Freud's notion of "grief work." Bonanno posits that in reality, human beings are psychologically well equipped for resilience. He estimates that only 10 to 15 percent of bereaved individuals are likely to struggle with enduring grief reactions that interfere with their ability to function in daily life.[18] That means most people are able to move forward with life, and even find happiness in spite of the grief they carry.

It feels a bit too reductive to me to say that grief is simply overcome by resilience. Frankly, I think it's almost impossible to explain the mysterious and sacred phenomenon of healing from grief. Once again, words fail us. The life of grief is learning to live with a peace that passes all understanding. It is learning to live with an affliction for which there is no cure. You integrate the wound into your daily life. You learn to live with a gaping hole in the world.

I feel that slowly, over time, I've developed some sense of agency, like the sorrow no longer controls me. Grief will always be unruly from time to time, but little by little it's become more and more tame. It's a bit like a domesticated cat now, and less like a roaring, prowling lion.

I've come to believe that just because I'm devastated doesn't mean I'm not coping well. Perhaps this is what Paul is getting at in 2 Corinthians 4 when he describes a life in which we are hard pressed, perplexed, persecuted, and struck down. We even carry death in our bodies, but it is the death of Jesus that eventually gives way to life. Yes, the pressure, persecution, and perplexity of life may continue, but we do not have to be crushed by it. We are not endlessly despairing. We are not abandoned. We are not destroyed.

Mary Oliver, in her poem "Heavy," states:

> *It's not the weight you carry*
> *but how you carry it—*
> *books, bricks, grief—*[19]

She goes on to write that embracing the burden of grief requires practice and a sense of balance, much like bearing any other physical burden. It also necessitates a keen attention to both the sorrow *and* the joy that invade our grief-filled lives.

Wendell Berry writes in *Hannah Coulter*:

> I began to know my story then. Like everybody's it was going to be the story of living in the absence of the dead. What is the thread that holds it all together? Grief, I thought for a while. And grief is there sure enough…But grief is not a force and has no power to hold. You only bear it. Love is what carries you, for it is always there, even in the dark, or most in the dark, but shining out at times like gold stitches in a piece of embroidery.[20]

I'm not sure I would put this weight down even if I could. I think of the people I've lost. I loved them. I still love them. To say it was easy or that I was past it would be to diminish the love we shared. Because of my love for them, I will endure the long, slow, plodding toll of grief.

CHAPTER 10

FUNERAL GAMES

(JOY)

*I commend the enjoyment of life, because
there is nothing better for a person under the
sun than to eat and drink and be glad.*

—Ecclesiastes 8:15

Once I was visiting an aid worker compound in Juba, South Sudan. The world's youngest nation had languished under the weight of famine, political violence, tribal warfare, and a failing economy since its founding in 2011. Our organization was one of hundreds of NGOs seeking to provide assistance. Our South Sudanese and expatriate staff were doing amazing work through food programs, clean water projects, and leadership development. But they shared with me that many days, the labor felt like a drop in the bucket.

Scrawled on the whiteboard in one of the cramped offices of the compound was a quote from Frederick Buechner: "Here is the world. Beautiful and terrible things will happen. Don't be afraid."

Beautiful and terrible. It's true in South Sudan. It's true everywhere. As I type this, I am watching unimaginable scenes of desperation play out at the Kabul airport. Afghanistan is seventy-two hundred miles away from my little home in the mountains of North Carolina, but it feels as close as a heartbeat thanks to my television, the internet, and the faithful work of journalists there.

These days, the sorrow of an entire world is at our fingertips. We spend our days scrolling through headlines and images of suffering from across the globe. We live in constant cognitive proximity to the world's greatest disasters. On the one hand, there is a blessing in the exposure that globalization has gained for those in need. We are able to advocate, vote, give, and pray in ways that are unprecedentedly informed. But on the other hand, I wonder sometimes if our hearts were meant to know *so much*. Each of us carries our own personal sorrows, great and small, trivial and significant. When you add the weight of the world's sorrows to that, our compassion can easily be fatigued beyond capacity. Physiologically, it is a lot to bear. How do you wrap your brain around it all, bring your beating heart to care for all the pain there is in this beautiful, terrible world?

The temptation of course is to numb, to steel yourself into feeling nothing, to become like Teflon so nothing is absorbed and everything rolls off you. But, as Brené Brown has been so good to remind us, we cannot selectively numb.[1] To choose numbness is to disregard all the wonder and mystery and pleasure this world has to offer.

To choose numbness is not the way of God, who was so brokenhearted by the sin of the world that He chose to put on skin and step directly into the sorrow. God was powerfully committed to His grief. He subjected Himself to the world's worst pain in order to redeem us and rescue His creation. Numbness was not the way of Jesus, who was so moved with compassion that He touched the untouchables, fed exhausted crowds even when He Himself was exhausted, and washed the feet of those who would go on to abandon Him.

Nicholas Wolterstorff writes, "The Stoics of antiquity said: Be calm. Disengage yourself. Neither laugh nor weep. Jesus says: Be open to the wounds of the world. Mourn humanity's mourning, weep over humanity's weeping, be wounded by humanity's wounds, be in agony over humanity's agony. But do so in the good cheer that a day of peace is coming."[2]

There are certainly times when good cheer feels impossible. Our ancestors understood this. The history of mourning is replete with rituals of sadness. But there are also some incredible rituals of joy to be found in the midst of mourning.

• • • • •

Book 23 of the Iliad begins with a scene of grief. Achilles and the Myrmidons are mourning the death of their beloved friend and comrade Patroclus. After a period of weeping and wailing aloud, the men partake of a feast and prepare a funeral pyre for the body of Patroclus. Then, they begin to play games.

The funeral games of the Iliad consisted of chariot races, boxing, wrestling, footraces, archery, and spear throwing. In the course of the competition, there was trash talk, laughter, bitter rivalry, and intervention from the gods. Achilles presided over the games and distributed gifts and prizes to the winners of the various events. All of this transpired a mere two days after the grief-stricken Achilles led his men in mourning.

> All as one
>> the armies cried out in sorrow, and Achilles led the
>>> chant.
> Three times they drove their full-maned stallions round
>> the body,
> Myrmidon soldiers mourning, and among them Thetis
>> stirred
>> a deep desire to grieve. And the sands grew wet,
>> the armor of fighting men grew wet with tears,
>> such bitter longing he roused.[3]

Funeral games were common in Greek and Roman antiquity. Some scholars believe that the ritual may have been a type of combat trial, in which the man responsible for the death of the deceased could be punished. In this way, the games would have been seen to appease the anger of the one who had died.[4] Certainly the games were a way to honor the dead. But other scholars note that funeral games were a mechanism by which the mourners could process their loss. Historian David Potter writes, "Funeral games are not just about saying farewell to the dead; they may also enable the survivors to reintegrate without the vital presence of the person whose departure they are lamenting."[5] Through funeral games, the bereaved are able to see that diversion, sport, and laughter continue even after the loved one is gone. They experience their own vigor and energy returning.

The Greco-Roman world was not the only culture in history to embrace revelry after a death. It was customary in many European cultures, particularly those with Celtic roots, to keep a constant vigil over the body from the moment of death until the burial. The deceased was never to be left alone. Watchers would sit up all night, and sometimes multiple nights, with the body and comfort the grieving family. In the days before medical doctors or coroners, it was important to keep a close watch to ensure that the person was, in fact, dead. While a *watching* was a solemn affair, the long tedious hours of keeping vigil required some amusement. Certainly an abundance of food and drink helped toward this end.[6]

There are records from the fourteenth century that speak of watchers who sought to relieve their boredom by "rousing the ghost." This activity seems to have consisted of playing practical jokes meant to frighten superstitious family members. It often involved moving the corpse. Some think these games may harken back to the even older tradition of attempting to raise the dead via black magic. These frivolities must have been a common occurrence because the Council of York, held in 1367, issued a statement condemning "those guilty games and follies, and all those perverse customs which transformed a house of tears and prayers into a house of laughing and excess."[7]

The Irish are perhaps the most notorious for their custom of holding lively wakes. It is thought that the residents of the Emerald Isle have been amusing themselves at funerals for as long as a millennium. In Ireland, a wake could officially begin after neighbor women had washed the body and covered it in white linen. Next came the keening, the explicit permission to wail demonstratively over the loss of the loved one. The midnight rosary was the cue that the merrymaking could begin.[8]

Wake games took many forms, and people from all over the community would come to participate. For the family of the departed, the tension of the lead-up to and finalization of death was released. The exhaustion of worry and caretaking gave way to outbursts of silliness and imprudence. Practical jokes were common, such as mixing pepper with tobacco, tying shoelaces together, and stitching old men's coats to chairs. Neighbor boys would hide under the bed of the corpse and shake it violently, causing quite a scare. Word games, hide-and-seek, and games of dare were enjoyed.

The lost loved one was honored and remembered. Stories from the deceased's younger days and memories of happier times flowed freely from the lips of the bereaved, fueled by generous portions of alcohol. Actors would mimic the gestures and voice of the dead.[9] Laughter and tears mingled together in a cacophony of mirth and sorrow.

Playacting and pantomime were a popular part of the Irish wake. A young man would often serve as the master of ceremonies. This leader, known as a *cleasai* in Irish, would pretend to be the local priest and take fellow revelers' "confessions." Sometimes, a marrying game was played where wives were chosen for men and mock ceremonies were performed. In some cases, wakes would take on a licentious nature, with lewd jokes and sexual exploits pursued in the dark of the night.[10]

The tradition of wake merriment carried over into southern Appalachia, perhaps due to the large Irish immigrant population in the area. Often, young men were obliged to stay up all night with the body. These young men, in turn, would ask certain young ladies, whom they were interested in, to sit up with them, transforming the whole event into an impromptu date. After midnight, when the old folks went to bed, the girls would fix a meal for the boys, and the whole gang would crowd into the kitchen, playing games, laughing, courting, and making candy into the wee hours of the morning. A few would even sneak off to the hayloft.[11]

The sexual nature of wake games is fairly scandalous to our modern sensibilities. It may seem misplaced to brazenly pursue romantic and sensual gratification in the presence of a corpse and a wailing keener. What is it about a wake that inspires such spirited flirtation and the shirking off of decorum? Writer and filmmaker Kevin Toolis, who remembers participating in wake games as a teenager in rural Ireland, writes this:

> By acting out, playing games around the corpse, the *cleasai* helped unleash some of our own deepest longings. The coldness of a corpse has its own perverse existential aphrodisiac; nothing so encourages the animal within us, the hunger for sexual consummation, need of the comfort of another warm body, than the death's present denial. We affirm ourselves in heat and flesh.[12]

Toolis's scandalous assessment may feel vulgar, but I understand what he is getting at. Whether it is the fear of death or the existential weight of death's crushing finality, our response to a corpse can trigger a personal moment of carpe diem. In the tangible presence of mortality, there emerges a sense of urgency to seize the day, to taste and experience everything this wild and beautiful life has to offer us as long as our souls inhabit these physical, feeling bodies. This is the kind of hedonism only death can conjure.

• • • • •

I used to make up things about my grief. I used to tell myself that my losses weren't that bad, that I was going to be just fine. I'd say that my grandmother was old and we were prepared for her to die. I'd remind myself that we hadn't yet picked out a name for our baby, so we weren't that attached or invested yet. I'd tell myself that my sister and I talked on the phone only once every couple of weeks and saw each other only once every two or three months, so her absence might not be that noticeable. I'd tell myself that I had a beautiful little girl already, so a miscarriage was no big deal.

I needed my life to fit into a category, to feel like things were "all good" and everything was going to be okay. I was scared that all the difficulties I'd experienced meant that my life henceforth was going to be categorically bad.

What is this propensity in us to be so unwilling to admit that something is truly, totally, and spectacularly awful? I've come to believe that the best thing you can do in grief is tell yourself the truth. Every bit of it. Death is hard and ugly and unnatural.

But if we tell ourselves the truth about the bad, we must also tell ourselves the truth about the good. No, we will not be miserable forever. In fact, we may experience powerful and profound glimpses of joy even in our darkest days of grief. The cognitive dissonance of this both/and life is as inspiring as it is confounding.

I suppose life would be easier in some ways if we could categorize it simply as either good or bad. But it's not that simple. The bad things that happen do not lessen the beauty of the good things. And the good things that happen do not negate the pain of the bad things. They both exist side by side. It's not a competition.

Some of the placating lies I told myself about my grief were just silly. Others, frankly, were obscene. For me, freedom came only when I finally embraced the idea that yes, *this is as awful as you* can imagine. *It's as bad as you think it is.* Then came an *and*, not a *but.* The additional, necessary truths that buoyed me up out of the waves of grief were not truths that diminished what had happened, but rather truths that equipped me to navigate my way through the crisis. Truths like this: My sister is gone. *And* I have good friends I can lean on. Life is so hard right now. *And* God is here. Our baby's heart stopped beating. *And* little Jane just took her first steps. I'm utterly devastated. *And* I will feel joy again.

I picture it like a boat way out at sea that finds itself caught up in a hurricane. You could lie to yourself and say the winds aren't so strong, the waves not that high, the danger not so great. Or you could say, "This is a terrible storm…*and* I have a radio. I have my navigation tools. I have a life preserver." And, of course, "It is very likely that the sun will someday shine again."

I can think of no other tradition in the world that more effectively holds the competing truths of life than the Irish wake. Two leading figures at the wake provide permission for us to step fully into the broad spectrum of our humanity. The *bean chaointe*, who leads in the keening serves as a midwife to our sorrow. The *cleasai* rouses the crowd to boisterous joy. Permission to be fully human is granted. All in one night, in one house, in one space.

It reminds me of a passage in the Old Testament book of Ezra. The people of God have returned to Jerusalem after a long and painful exile, and they are seeking to rebuild the temple of the Lord. "But many of the older priests and Levites and family heads, who had seen the former temple, wept aloud when they saw the foundation of this temple being laid, while many others shouted for joy. No one could distinguish the sound of the shouts of joy from the sound of weeping, because the people made so much noise. And the sound was heard far away" (Ezra 3:12–13).

The ever-present weight of memory. The hope of what is to come. There is no distinction. It is all woven together. The frightening and beautiful noise of it all resounds across the miles and miles of our years. In this tension, this *both/and*, we live and move and have our being, all in the presence of a God who also sobs and sings.

· · · · ·

I'm not the only weary, burned-out millennial who has had a revelatory experience stumbling upon the book of Ecclesiastes. When I found it in my early thirties, this set of wisdom writings from the teacher Qoheleth, the sage king, felt like it had been buried in my Bible for years. Perhaps I'd avoided it because of the dismal nature of the introduction: "'Meaningless! Meaningless!' says the Teacher. 'Utterly meaningless! Everything is meaningless!'" (Eccl. 1:2). This didn't exactly square with my American evangelical commitment to Christocentric positivity.

Qoheleth's writings pull no punches when it comes to doubt, disillusionment, and the creeping sense of futility that come with age. These sentiments are near and dear to the heart of any proper millennial. Frankly, this exhaustion of life is a universal human experience, so when I rediscovered this book a few years ago, I had the profound sense of being lost and found, of being seen and affirmed.

Qoheleth reminds us that there is nothing new under the sun. There is no silver bullet to eliminate our inadequacies, our dissatisfactions, or our mortality. With wisdom comes much sorrow; with pleasure and wealth comes disappointment; with toil come fatigue and restlessness. We sow seeds, but, very often, we reap thorns and thistles. The ground of our labor is cursed. Those who embrace wisdom and those who pursue folly both face the same fate. We all go to the grave, and the riches we've acquired will pass on to another. And who knows whether or not they will squander the fruit of the sweat of our brow. Nothing endures. Everything is chasing after the wind.

But in chapter 2, verse 24, Qoheleth introduces an intriguing solution to the disillusionment: "A person can do nothing better than to eat and drink and find satisfaction in their own toil. This too, I see, is from the hand of God." This same sentiment is expressed multiple times through the remainder of the book, in chapter 3, verses 12, 13, and 22; in chapter 5, verses 17 and 18; in chapter 8, verse 15; and in chapter 9, verses 7 through 9. It's a *resounding* theme: Enjoy life when you can because our lot is hard. Savor good food and drink, enjoy the affection of your lover, and revel in the satisfaction of a hard day's work. As Ecclesiastes 8:15 says, "I commend the enjoyment of life, because there is nothing better for a person under the sun than to eat and drink and be glad. Then joy will accompany them in their toil all the days of the life God has given them under the sun."

The thought that I could be accompanied by joy as I walk through the pain and toil of life is deeply hopeful. It is almost as if the antidote to sorrow is savoring. While obviously framed in light of the final "conclusion" of the whole matter, outlined in 12:13 ("Fear God and keep his commandments"), this holy hedonism is commended to us by one of the wisest teachers who ever lived.

When I went to school at a Christian college and majored in Bible and philosophy, I was warned against the salacious worldview of hedonism. Hedonism is a theory of motivation that asserts the intention behind any act is, or should be, pleasure. The Greek word translated as "pleasure" is *hedone*. It's important to remember that many of history's most prominent hedonists, such as Epicurus, advocated not for drunkenness, gluttony, or lechery, but rather for the prudent pursuit of freedom from fear and anxiety.[13] Epicurus, like Qoheleth, believed in the importance of virtue and some measure of inhibition. Nevertheless, when most of us think of the concept of hedonism, we picture wild, booze-fueled parties, unrestrained sexual exploits, and a rejection of all moral and social obligations. This lifestyle, we are told, is to be flatly rejected by the committed believer. We are cautioned to avoid anyone who lives by the axiom "Eat, drink, and be merry, for tomorrow we die."

So what do we do with the hedonistic undertones we find in Ecclesiastes? Some biblical teachers and scholars in recent years have developed the concept of Christian hedonism, in which a person experiences maximum joy and pleasure by basking in the glory of God. As John Piper says, "God is most glorified in us when we are most satisfied in him."[14]

I don't reject this notion at all. But I also think there is something uniquely Christian about the ability to truly savor *all* of God's good gifts. These good gifts include not only His presence and glory but also something as simple as the sweetness of an apple, the beauty of a spring flower, the warmth of an embrace, and the majesty of the mountains. We forget that the maxim "Eat, drink, and be merry" was drawn from the wise words of Qoheleth in Ecclesiastes 8:15. It is possible to fear God, to keep His commandments, *and*, as Henry David Thoreau challenges us, to "suck all the marrow of life."

Jesus, even though He had stepped entirely and wholeheartedly into the pain and suffering of the world, strikes me as the kind of person who sought to savor the good things His Father's earth had to offer. In the Scriptures, we often find Him at dinner parties, drinking, eating, and talking. We see Him wandering the hills and spending time with friends.

I could be wrong, but I think it gives God great delight when we experience the physical pleasures of this world. After all, wasn't it David who wrote in Psalm 30:11, "You turned my wailing into dancing; you removed my sackcloth and clothed me with joy"? Isaiah proclaims to the poor, the brokenhearted, and the bereaved that God has bestowed on them "a crown of beauty instead of ashes, the oil of joy instead of mourning, and a garment of praise instead of a spirit of despair" (Isa. 61:3).

No virtue in the world seems as righteous and life-giving as the virtue of thankfulness. *That*, to me, is at the core of Christian hedonism, the awe-filled recognition of all the marvelous things God has given us. If anything, grief increases our capacity to be thankful. The good things in life taste sweeter when we have tasted the bitterness of death.

This ritual of savoring was something I committed myself to while I was in the throes of grief. I was determined to reclaim my ability to love my life again.

• • • • •

It has been a powerful experience writing about my deepest sadness even as I have finally had the joy of welcoming two healthy baby girls into the world. The sorrow of grief and the delight of motherhood occurring in jagged synchronicity made it impossible to succinctly categorize the quality of my life as either good or bad. It was good *and* bad. Of all the labors I have ever undertaken, the labor of giving life and the labor of grieving life have by far been the holiest. To grieve is indeed a labor, a birthing of something new in us. It is travail.

One of my favorite poems is Kahlil Gibran's "On Joy and Sorrow." In it, he writes:

Your joy is your sorrow unmasked.
And the selfsame well from which your laughter rises
was oftentimes filled with your tears.
And how else can it be?
The deeper that sorrow carves into your being,
the more joy you can contain.[15]

I can't decide if I've mastered the art of harboring in my soul two extraordinarily contrasting emotions. Sometimes when I look at my daughters, I feel my heart stretching toward them with an overwhelming love, but then my head puts me in check, that powerful impulse to love instinctively stymied by the deep caution that grief has embedded in me.

But then there are times when I think my love for them is actually *more* sublime because of all the hurt I've experienced. As Jerry Sittser writes, "Loss can diminish us, but it can also expand us."[16] People tend to think of grief as the ultimate deficit maker, that it forever debilitates you from experiencing the goodness of life. This may be true for a time. But in the long haul of the grief journey, your ability to appreciate what is good in the world doesn't have to be decreased. In fact, I believe it can be increased.

Sittser puts it this way: "The soul is elastic, like a balloon. It can grow larger through suffering. Loss can enlarge its capacity for anger, depression, despair, and anguish, all natural and legitimate emotions whenever we experience loss. Once enlarged, the soul is also capable of experiencing greater joy, strength, peace, and love."[17] Grief uniquely outfits us to experience the joys of life.

My soul has grown to accommodate both my grief and my love. Nicholas Wolterstorff writes,

To believe in Christ's rising and death's dying is also to live with the power and the challenge to rise up now from all our dark graves of suffering love. If sympathy for the world's wounds is not enlarged by our anguish, if love for those around us is not expanded, if gratitude for what is good does not flame up, if insight is not deepened, if commitment to what is important is not strengthened, if aching for a new day is not intensified, if hope is weakened and faith diminished, if from the experience of death comes nothing good, then death has won. Then death, be proud.[18]

I won't give death another inch. I won't dignify it by allowing it to rob me of one more moment of joy, of awe, of gratefulness. I won't remain numb. If death is proud, then let my joy be prouder, stronger, more tenacious. Let it be inimitable. The ultimate act of resistance is to enjoy life, to savor it with every bit of strength I have left in me, to eat, drink, and be merry. We must feast on life. As Mary Oliver writes: "If you suddenly and unexpectedly feel joy, don't hesitate. Give in to it…don't be afraid of its plenty. Joy is not made to be a crumb."[19]

•　•　•　•　•

Like the ancient Greeks, I long to honor the memory of the person I've lost. And I've begun to think that embracing life and living it to the fullest is one of the most important ways I can honor her. I don't honor her by ignoring the pain. But I also don't honor her by ignoring the joy forever. My happiness runs parallel to my sadness, and the key is to learn to live with and truly honor both feelings.

In *The Odyssey*, Homer writes of the person who has endured suffering: "Even his griefs are a joy long after to one that remembers all that he wrought and endured." I'm not sure I agree fully with Homer on this statement. I'm not sure you can ever call true grief a joy. It will always be a grief. It will always be painful. Yes, there are good things that will happen after my sister's death, perhaps even good things that would not have been possible had she not died. But that does not make her death good. It just doesn't. Her death will never be anything but truly awful.

I don't think there's some grand cosmic scale in which all the good we've experienced suddenly outweighs the bad. I don't think our lives work like a bank account, where catastrophes make withdrawals and blessings make deposits and you sit down at the end of your days hoping that somehow you've ended up in the black. Life always outgrows all our tidy metaphors. It is never either in the red or in the black. It's always both.

But I can say that I do look back on my griefs with a sense of awe. It's an awe that I wouldn't categorize as happiness or relief or even redemption. It's a wonder-filled awe, a breathtaking kind of awe. It's amazement that we persevered, that God was there, that we rose to that awful occasion, broken though our wings may have been. It's a deep sense of reverence for the people who showed up in our lives in powerful ways when we needed them. It's an amazement at the hard-fought resilience that was wrought over time with love and tears and terror. And yes, perhaps it is a joy, in seeing the stubborn persistence of tenderness, and life's ability to keep handing us beauty even after all feels lost.

CHAPTER 11

DEATH ROOMS

(MORTALITY)

Teach us to number our days,
that we may gain a heart of wisdom.

—Psalm 90:12

We live between two graveyards. A few doors down to the left sits Hopewell Church with a large fenced-in grassy knoll containing a couple hundred stone markers. This cemetery remains neatly kept by landscapers, and there are still several burials that take place there each year. A few doors down to the right of our house is the Blackburn family graveyard at what was once the site of the Blackburn family homestead and original Hopewell Church building. Trees hang low over the grave sites. Roots have cracked and upended the stone markers, most of which are too rubbed down by time and weather to read. A few kindhearted neighbors run a weed eater over the graves several times a year, but by all accounts, this graveyard is not far from succumbing to the overgrowth.

On any given evening, Jane and I will walk down our driveway to the road, and I'll ask her which way she wants to walk. Whichever way she chooses, a graveyard is the destination. She meanders giggling through the moss-covered headstones and examines the carvings: a rose for a beloved mother, a Scripture passage, a lamb for a little child, a finger pointing toward the sky.

These hills are dotted with small cemeteries. Early Appalachian families would bury their dead high up on ridges, areas too steep for building homes or farming. These grassy slopes that served as the resting place for loved ones towered over homes, barns, and gardens. Family cemeteries often grew to become community cemeteries where kin and neighbors were laid to rest together. Some graveyards were placed next to a church, or sometimes a church was built next to a graveyard. Communities would worship, get married, go to school, and meet for socials all within sight of the dead. Mortality was always on the purview. As my friend Justin Lonas, who also lives next to a cemetery, writes, "In every season, the cemetery is a present, patient, faithful *memento mori* that demands it not be passed off as a mere park."[1]

Beliefs about the proper place to bury the dead have changed throughout history. Most cultures of antiquity regarded corpses as unclean, so places of burial were generally far removed from the community, most often outside the city walls. This changed when Christendom began to expand. The belief in the resurrection of the body and the veneration of martyrs and their tombs created a comfort, even an enthusiasm for the nearness of burial sites. Cemeterial basilicas honoring the dead were constructed and later became central hubs for powerful abbeys. Residential communities grew up around these basilicas and pretty soon, every church, whether inside or outside the city walls, made space for the dead.[2] Seventeenth-century ecclesiastical writer Louis Thomassin wrote,

> Since the Son of God has not only sanctified, but crucified death itself, not only in his own person but in his members, not only by his own resurrection but by the hope he gives to us, by the instilling in our mortal bodies his quickening spirit, which is the source of eternal life, the tombs of those who died for him have been regarded as sources of life and sanctity. This is why they have been placed in churches.[3]

But the churchyard burial ground fell out of favor for many reasons. As populations grew, graveyards became overcrowded. Some burials were five or six coffins deep. Floods would sometimes break walls and coffins would crack open. During epidemics, graveyards were seen as breeding grounds for diseases. It was decided that the dead, once again, should be moved outside the city where there was plenty of space. In fact, these early memorial parks were designed at a time when there were few public parks for leisure and relaxation. People used to go to these cemeteries and enjoy the fragrant gardens and artistic sculptures. They would host hunting and sporting events there. People would picnic among the dead, play among the dead, and sip tea among the dead.[4]

These days we rarely play football or baseball at cemeteries. We are more like our ancestors of antiquity. Whether we admit it or not, the dead seem unclean, uncomfortable. They remain in a realm far removed from our living spaces. We visit graveyards infrequently, for a burial, or maybe the anniversary of a death.

Unless you are like little Jane, who likes to play hide-and-seek among the tombstones.

• • • • •

During the last century the dead have not only been relegated to parks outside the city walls. The whole process of dying, from illness to interment, has been outsourced to hospitals and funeral homes. This became abundantly clear to me in my study of grief rituals, but it took me some time to understand how and when this change in our engagement with death and the dying occurred.

Early Christians were the first to establish institutions similar to what we now know as hospitals. These were places of hospitality designed to care for the sick and the dying who had been abandoned by society. They also provided assistance in the way of food and shelter to widows, orphans, and the poor. Monasteries sometimes added wards to treat and tend to the sick and, later, institutions arose to quarantine and house people with contagious diseases.[5]

For most of history, hospitals were a place only the destitute or abandoned went to for medical help. If a person became ill, care was typically rendered by family members using folk medicine or home remedies. The wealthy could afford to have servants provide assistance or could possibly pay for a doctor to conduct a home visit. Doctors were mobile and made house calls to treat sick people in their own bedrooms, in their own beds. But as medical sophistication grew, families dispersed, and capitalism monetized health care, there was a gradual shift to the institution of medicine within the walls of a designated facility. According to Dr. Lydia S. Dugdale, in 1873, there existed fewer than two hundred hospitals in the United States. By 1920, there were more than six thousand.[6] Hospitals are now the place where we come into the world and the place where we go out of it.

The first home Tim and I ever bought together was a small brick cottage in a wooded hollow—or "holler," as they say here—about ten minutes from Boone. Just down the road from us was an old cabin inhabited by a ninety-four-year-old named Miss Mary. She had never married and so she lived there on her own after her father passed away. She cooked on a woodstove and, having no indoor plumbing, fetched her water from a well and used an outhouse.

Miss Mary was a sweet lady who had a spry sense of humor, a love for Coca-Cola and banjo music, and a fear of hospitals and medicine. On our first visit, she pointed to the antique bed and said, "I was born right over there in that corner," and she smiled. "Don't worry, I've changed the bed since then!" Several years after we met her, at the ripe old age of ninety-eight, she died as she had requested: at home, in the same cabin where she had been born.

Miss Mary is in the minority. These days, only 1 out of 5 Americans die at home.[7]

The funeral industry began to grow around the same time that hospital usage was expanding. Between 1850 and 1950, people began to believe that caring for the dead was something only a professional could do. This was in large part due to the growth in the popularity of embalming, a practice that was never before embraced so extensively in the Western world. In the past, the vast majority of people who died were simply washed and dressed prior to being buried. That all changed during the Civil War.

Between 1861 and 1865, hundreds of thousands of soldiers

died miles and miles away from their homes. Many were simply left on the battlefields where they fell or piled into mass graves. But some prominent families made arrangements to have their fallen loved ones returned home to be properly mourned and buried.[8] The practice of chemical embalming, which had been developed in the early part of the nineteenth century for the purpose of preserving bodies for scientific study, made this possible.

Embalming grew in popularity during and immediately after the Civil War, with undertakers becoming the primary practitioners. Chemical companies and casket makers capitalized on the growing demand, and full-fledged institutes that taught embalming techniques arose. In 1882, the first meeting of the National Funeral Directors Association took place.[9] Now, no other country in the world embalms the dead at a rate even close to that of the US.[10]

Before the turn of the century, funeral directors would often conduct the embalming in homes, and so the dead continued to be displayed in living spaces for visiting family and friends. At some point, many funeral directors began to open their own homes for embalming and visitations, and eventually what we know as the modern-day funeral parlor or funeral home was born.[11]

Funeral directors now take great pride in providing an atmosphere of calm serenity where a family can view the dead and friends can visit and pay their respects before a funeral. Visitations typically last no more than two hours and are conducted either the night before or just prior to a funeral service. After the service, a funeral director and his assistants close the casket lid, wheel the body out into a hearse, and drive it to the cemetery, where it is set up on a lowering device to be put into the ground after a brief graveside service.

This total outsourcing of death to the industries of medicine and funeral homes has, I fear, inadvertently led to the deeply held notion that we do our living in our homes, but we do our dying somewhere else. Somewhere far away. We live with our families, but we die with a doctor. We live in community, but we are buried outside the walls of the city. We ignore death as long as we can, until we are abruptly confronted with it and somehow have to deal with it. And then we pay through the nose to not have to look at it, to hear it, to smell it. The average cost of a funeral in America is between $6,000 and $9,000.[12]

• • • • •

In 1963, Jessica Mitford published *The American Way of Death*, a scathing exposé of the funeral business in the United States. It became a surprise best seller and led to congressional hearings on the funeral industry. She was deeply critical of funeral directors and claimed they monetize death, taking advantage of grief-stricken mourners, convincing them to pay a fortune to honor their loved ones.

I actually deeply respect the work of funeral directors. They have the courage and fortitude to embrace a vocation that revolves around death. I don't blame them for our loss of rituals or our distaste for the reality of mortality. In fact, I appreciate the ways in which they seek to preserve our few remaining rituals of mourning and honor lost loved ones and their families. As with anything, it's hard to know if funeral directors adjusted their practices to accommodate changes in society's desires or if their actions actually molded those desires. Either way, they do what many of us are afraid to do: tangibly encounter mortality and suffering on a daily basis.

I am also incredibly thankful for hospitals. When I was eighteen, I developed a life-threatening inflammation of the colon, and had it not been for my access to a hospital, I probably would have died. All kinds of people, young and old, have brushes with death. Doctors and nurses working in the hospital context with the tools of modern medicine are able to treat and cure, adding years, sometimes decades, to our lives. Sometimes we go to the hospital to die because there's a possibility that we might *not* die.

I just wonder if, in losing the tactile, palpable nature of caring for the dying and the deceased within our own spaces of living, we have lost our grasp of the reality of death and grief. In the past, it was simply a given that loved ones and neighbors would carry the heavy burden of caring for the sick or the aged in their final days. In spite of the exhausting, putrid, demoralizing nature of that work, it was considered part of life, a duty that was expected and embraced. Once the end finally came, the body would remain in the home and be prepared by those same friends, family members, and neighbors. It was lovingly washed and dressed in shrouds or nice clothing. People didn't just "do life" together. They "did death" together as well.

In parts of Appalachia, bodies were laid out on what was called a "cooling board" or a "laying out board." The long, straight board was a good alternative to sunken-in mattresses, which caused the body to bow as rigor mortis set in. The cooling board was made of a hardwood and was about the size of a twin bed. It was placed on either two chairs or two sawhorses. The body was then stretched out straight onto the cooling board, and there it was prepared for burial. It was said that each family had a cooling board that was used by several generations and passed down through the family. When it wasn't being used to prepare a body, it was cleaned and used as a trestle table at church picnics or barn raisings.[13] Once again, we see the traditions of death and life woven together into a seamless tapestry.

It was common throughout the United States and Europe to leave the body on display for a period of time before the burial so that friends, neighbors, and relatives could pay their respects. Sometimes the body was left in a bedroom, covered in clean sheets, and surrounded by flowers. Oftentimes, the body was displayed in the front room or the parlor.

In the Victorian home the parlor was a formal space for receiving guests. It was where ceremonial family events took place, like weddings and holiday celebrations. It was also the place where bodies were displayed for visitation and wakes were held. Because of the frequency of death in those times, some people even think the parlor may have been referred to as the "death room." According to legend, the term "living room" emerged from an article published in the *Ladies' Home Journal* in the early 1900s. The article suggested that with decreasing mortality rates, the front parlor should no longer be a death room but should be a place for the living, a space where families should relax and forgo formalities. And so, the fable says, the modern-day living room was born.[14]

Funeral parlors eventually aided to this end by providing an alternative place to display a body and receive visitors. Death had officially moved out of our living spaces. Dugdale writes that sometime in the 1950s, "death came to replace sex as the ultimate 'unmentionable.'…Death was sequestered from public view and dismissed as a subject of polite conversation. Doctors failed to mention it. Families failed to witness it. The hospital promised to conquer it."[15] The death room no longer exists within the walls of our homes, and mortality no longer occupies our consciousness. The speakable has become unspeakable.

As children, we proceed through life untrained in the ways of death and grief. Before I went to Iraq, I could probably count on one hand the number of dead bodies I'd seen. In the last one hundred years, as the average age of death rose significantly, perhaps the need to educate people on how to handle death seemed less urgent. Somehow death, while it is the inevitable fate of every human being, seems so…*rare*. Uncommon. Out of the ordinary. Watching a baby, watching a teenager, and watching an old man at our field hospital die was surreal and horrifying to me, not just because war was foreign to me, but also because death was foreign to me.

The worst moments of my life have taken place either in a hospital room or in a funeral home. Everyone present—the doctors, the nurses, the funeral directors—all did their best to create as safe a space around my personal tragedies as they could. I listened to them go through a mental Rolodex of polite statements, things you say during times of crisis: "Unfortunately, we have no options left. I'm so sorry for your loss. May I request a visit from the chaplain? Everything is in order. I think you'll find her appearance quite pleasing and peaceful." They did the best they could, but there is no fixing what is so terribly broken. Kindness and professionalism are all you can bring to moments like that, and I appreciated it. They made the necessary arrangements as I stumbled in my shock and grief across the thresholds of their spaces and back home to try to make sense of what had happened.

I'd prefer to keep those images, those smells, those sounds as far away from my everyday reality as I can. For me, death happened in a heavily curtained, thickly potpourried parlor with ambient worship music playing faintly in the background. It felt like a dream, like a sanitized, saccharine nightmare. And I just can't decide. Am I grateful for the sequestered nature of that experience? Or do I wish it had been stark? Blunt. Rank. Intrusive. Indecent. Would it have been a better reflection of reality? Because we can outsource a body to a mortician, but we cannot outsource our grief. We can put a corpse in a funeral home, but our grief goes with us wherever we go. It abides with us in our spaces of living.

And would allowing death into my everyday space help familiarize me, prepare me for next time? Prepare me for my own time?

• • • • •

The only poem of the psalter attributed to Moses is Psalm 90. This ancient, barefaced piece of writing is a meditation on the precarity, brevity, and wretchedness of life. Moses, who was born amid an infanticide, who knew what it was to take another man's life, who witnessed plague and pestilence, who buried his sister Miriam and his brother Aaron. Moses, who wandered with the wayward people of Israel for forty years in the wilderness and never reached the final destination. Moses knew death. He knew the bitterness of fruitless labor, the miscarriage of hope and purpose.

The poem is a list of contrasts, of Moses bemoaning the transient nature of human life and labor with the timeless dominion of God. Our sins are met with God's fury and our lives are snuffed out. The conclusion Moses reaches is that the root of wisdom is to acknowledge the transience of our time on earth: "Teach us to number our days, that we may gain a heart of wisdom" (Ps. 90:12). As James 4:15 reminds us centuries later in the New Testament, we are a mist. Only "if it is the Lord's will" do we live.

The other conclusion Moses comes to in Psalm 90 is that we should ask God for happiness. Outright. "Make us glad for as many days as you have afflicted us, for as many years as we have seen trouble" (v. 15). And "establish the work of our hands for us—yes, establish the work of our hands" (v. 17). If God can take life, then He can give it in abundance too. If He can raze our work, then He can root it and prosper it as well.

This psalm is humiliating from start to finish. Moses, a tired, defeated man who failed in his final mission, approaches the God of all glory, who existed before the mountains were born. Moses names his personal sin and the communal sins of Israel. He admits that we are but dust; cut grass, withered and dry. Then he begs, like a convicted criminal, for mercy and pity. He begs, like a child, for happiness. How shameful! How mortifying!

I've written before about the holy humiliation that I experienced with death and grief. To this day, it is this embarrassment that is the most perplexing emotion I've felt in response to death. I know this might sound strange and, frankly, I find it impossible to even describe. But I felt like a failure. I felt like I'd been caught unaware, like I'd been ambushed. I felt irresponsible somehow, like I'd let my guard down or been naive. I look at old pictures of my family—smiling, happy, and blissfully unaware of the catastrophe that would befall us. And I think, *We were so stupid.* We were such suckers. How did we not see it coming? Why weren't we prepared? Why didn't we build a bunker or something?

Tim likes to tease me because if ever I'm hosting a dinner party and the meal is a bit overdone, I like to announce garishly to the group: "I just want everyone to know that *I know* the food is burned!" The thought of serving a bad-tasting meal, of having broccoli in my teeth, or of having my pants zipper down *without* my knowledge is horrifying to me. I don't exactly mind failing, but I like to do it on my own terms, undergirded by my own self-awareness. The thought of being oblivious petrifies me.

But death plays by no rules and doesn't care how it might sully your reputation. No amount of self-awareness lessens its sting. It will come for you and the ones you love the most, whether you are oblivious or if you see it coming a million miles away.

Somehow, I've got to learn how to hold the lives of my loved ones openhandedly, as James reminds us to do, without constantly rehearsing their deaths in my mind. "Anxiety is inefficient," Tim is good to remind me. Anxiety demands that we experience the pain of a loss *before* it even happens and then again if and when it actually *does* happen. To *remember* our mortality without worrying requires a mental and emotional dexterity only the truly wise acquire.

Most of us struggle more to absorb the reality of our own impermanence than the impermanence of the people we love. We all live as if we are immortal. Even though I know in my head that death is real—that a car wreck or cancer or old age will take me out of this world—in my heart I live and operate as if I'm going to be the one person in history who is able to overcome death and live forever. I expect tomorrow to come again and again, on and on into eternity. The thought of my soul leaving my body is simply incomprehensible.

Maybe Moses, with all his failures, had learned that true understanding comes only with this holy humiliation that is mortality. This is why I'm convinced that the rituals of repentance—ash, wailing, sackcloth—*must* mirror the rituals of grief. Sin and death reduce us to a humiliating dependence on God and a dismantling of our own prideful ego. But there is wisdom in this. For isn't it better to surrender your life to the providence of a good and unfailing God than to a mere mortal?

So we pray. So we beg. *God, give us joy. Watch over us. Establish the work of our hands. Please, God. Please.*

· · · · ·

Other cultures throughout history have found creative ways to invite death into their lives and spaces of living. The Día de los Muertos, or the Day of the Dead, is recognized most significantly in Mexican culture. Observed on the first and second of November, dates that correspond with the Catholic celebration of All Saints' Day and All Souls' Day, the Day of the Dead is a holiday that honors loved ones who have died. Altars dedicated to the deceased are set up in homes and graves are visited. Funny stories and an abundance of food are shared. And while the purpose of the holiday is to remember the dead, there is a festive, joyful nature to it.

In America, every year we celebrate Halloween on the eve of All Saints' Day. As I write this, I'm sitting in a university library that has been decorated for Halloween. The checkout desk has been covered in spiderwebs, and bats and plastic skulls hang from the ceiling. Most people believe that our Halloween traditions are rooted in pagan Roman harvest festivals, Catholic observances of All Saints' and All Souls' Day, and the Celtic festival of Samhain, which recognizes summer's end and winter's beginning. Halloween as we know it embodies a more cartoonish version of death, with ghouls, goblins, ghosts, and witches. In America, we don't mind being periodically spooked, as long as we are being entertained in the process.

I remember how strange it was to experience Halloween so soon after my sister died. The Styrofoam tombstones that went up in people's yards and the skeletons that hung from people's porches were a cruel reminder of what I'd just experienced. I watched all the trick-or-treaters gorging on their candy and taking selfies in their costumes and I wanted to scream at them, "This is not a joke! *Death is for real!* Mortality is no party!"

We intermittently expose ourselves to death in movies and television shows. But I've heard from many people that their tolerance for violence or tragedy in their entertainment was greatly diminished after they experienced significant grief in their own lives. Television is inherently ill-suited to teach us to grieve. When death is on a screen, we can simply change the channel or swipe away the image. The discomfort passes and we move on with our lives. Not so with grief. No wonder our bodies experience such shock when we find that we cannot bypass or compartmentalize true sorrow.

There's an old folk song popular in Appalachia called "Oh Death." There is a bit of mystery surrounding the origins of the song, which was famously featured in the movie *O Brother, Where Art Thou?*. Many mountain folks assert it was written by a preacher named Lloyd Chandler, who claims the song was given to him in a vision from God after a weekend of "sinning and shining" in 1916.[16] At its core, the song is an exchange, a discussion between a dying person and Death himself. The traditional lyrics are as follows:

> *Well what is this that I can't see*
> *With icy hands takin' hold of me*
> *Well I am Death, none can excel*
> *I'll open the door to Heaven and Hell*
> *O, Death, O, Death*
> *Won't you spare me over 'til another year?*

The song resonated deeply with mountain communities, people who knew well the precarity of life that comes with living in the wilderness of the wild and windy highlands. Death was achingly familiar to them, and so through song, they found a way to approach death, to interact with it in an honest and open way.

This, to me, seems like the kind of relationship Moses is advocating for. It is an ever-present acknowledgment of our mortality, and an admittance of our need for mercy. Mercy from death. The mercy of God. Death should be approachable. It should be touchable, not like the untouchable corpses the ancients banished outside the city walls. Not like the obscured experience of a costumed, rowdy holiday. Not like the dreaded grief we displace from our living spaces and confine to a hospital room or a funeral parlor.

• • • • •

I've written critically at times of the role the church has played in dismantling our grief rituals. But Jesus Himself entrusted to the church one of the most powerful, holy, and enduring rituals of grief that the world has ever known when He broke the bread and poured the wine in the Upper Room the night before His death. "Do this in remembrance of me," He said (1 Cor. 11:24). But what are we remembering when we reenact this meal?

Through the ritual of Communion, we are remembering what is, to me, the most profound plot twist ever to be found in any religious tradition, divine chronicle, or sacred metanarrative. The all-powerful, all-knowing, all-consuming God subjected Himself to death. And not just death. A humiliating death on a cross. On that cross He bore the entirety of human history's sin and sorrow. God became a body and allowed that body to die. Golgotha was "the place of the skull." God was taken *outside* the walls of the Holy City of Jerusalem to be crucified. God died on the margins. God was put in the ground, out of sight. Our Apostles' Creed tells us He even descended into hell.

God's subjugation of His very self to death was what facilitated everlasting life for all of us. God's approach to death was what made death forever approachable for us! It is the profundity and sacredness of this truth that has led to the careful stewardship of the ritual of Communion throughout the ages. The particulars of the practice are not void of controversy and disagreement. But I find it comforting to know that this simple act of eating bread and drinking wine has persisted through religious wars, cultural upheaval, and global catastrophes. It persists because the story of a God who chose to identify with us in death is simply too beautiful to ignore. It's too unbelievable *not* to believe.

The church has other rituals that recognize mortality. We smear ashes on our foreheads every year at the start of Lent. We wear around our necks an instrument of execution. The cross of Christ and the ashes of Lent call us to bear in mind our own mortality as well as the call to lay down our own lives and make room for Christ's sanctifying work. They also serve to remind us that we need not fear death. Death has been conquered. We have been offered mercy. Ours is the resurrection and the life!

But God's ultimate defeat of death doesn't mean we don't dread death to some degree, that it doesn't devastate us when it takes one of our loved ones. God's unblinking confrontation with death *does* mean that we have hope. We never fully reconcile with death; maybe we just familiarize ourselves, expose ourselves in measured ways, similar to the inoculation of a virus. We build our ability to resist a total descent into darkness. We invite death into our spaces of living so it is no stranger to us when we ourselves go to die.

Death is part of life. Its cruelty is a reality we must accept. And until we die, we hope. We pray. We approach God. We beg. "God, make us glad for as many years as we have seen trouble." And, I believe, once we make an acquaintance with death, we can approach it with that same familiarity, the same audacity, the same hopeful request. We can sing, as my ancestors did, "O, Death, won't you spare me over 'til another year." Please?

CHAPTER 12

DECORATION DAY

(HONOR)

*Praise be to the God and Father of our Lord
Jesus Christ, the Father of compassion and the
God of all comfort, who comforts us in all our
troubles, so that we can comfort those in any
trouble with the comfort we ourselves receive
from God.*

—2 Corinthians 1:3–4

Epicurus believed that the reason the living should not fear death was that in dying, we cease to exist and therefore won't experience the pain or turmoil of the death itself. He writes, "Accustom yourself to the belief that death is of no concern to us…While we exist death is not present, and when death is present we no longer exist. It is therefore nothing either to the living or to the dead since it is not present to the living, and the dead no longer are."[1]

I'm typically pretty dismissive of anyone who tells me that death is nothing to fear. But I know better than to argue with a dead philosopher, and in some respects, I can see where he is coming from. Certainly, death seems to exact its most painful wounding on the living who remain behind in their grief. Poet Owen Dodson captures this so poignantly:

> *Death always happens*
> *To somebody else,*
> *Not the dead.*[2]

Who is the "somebody else?" Friends, sisters, brothers, parents. It is the "survivors" who suffer through the shock, the pain of the absence, the lingering questions, and the regrets that come with death. My sister and my grandmother were spared from experiencing the agonizing aftermath of their own passing. We were not.

And yet, there's something about grief that can, at times, feel a bit selfish. It may sound strange, but when we lost my sister, I always felt like she, as the person who had died, should be at the center of the story. She was the primary victim. Her loss could never be about me or my pain. Her life, her legacy—that's what mattered the most.

As I've continued on in my broken, bereaved state, these are questions I've wrestled with: What is my responsibility to the dead? How do I honor their memories, or "keep their flame alive"? I've sometimes worried that if I don't *manage* the memory of my grandmother or my sister well, if I don't caretake their legacy, that somehow they will totally disappear. I cling desperately to any scrap of their existence. In spite of how incapacitated I am by my sadness, I've felt like my new full-time job is to never, ever let the world forget them. And somehow, no matter how much I strive, I feel them slipping further and further away.

• • • • •

Memorial Day in America, recognized on the last Monday of May, was officially established as a government holiday in 1968. The holiday as we know it today recognizes all American military personnel who have died in the line of duty. Initially, Memorial Day began as a commemoration of Civil War soldiers and was observed on different dates by various Southern and Northern states. It was sometimes known as Decoration Day.

Decoration Day in the Upland South, particularly Appalachia, however, is a distinctive tradition unique to this region in which *all* graves, military and civilian alike, within a particular cemetery are annually cleaned and adorned with flowers. Each family or church cemetery observes Decoration Day on a different but preestablished date on the calendar. Scholars maintain differing opinions on the origins of this unique mountain tradition. Some believe Decoration Day in southern Appalachia finds its roots in the Welsh holiday called "Flowering Sunday" during which flowers are strewn across graves on the same day as Palm Sunday.[3]

Others believe that the practice most likely grew out of the custom of *funeralizing*. Back when mountain settlements were remote and difficult to access, qualified members of the clergy were hard to come by. Often, funerals were delayed until a circuit preacher was available to come to the isolated community and conduct the service. A person would be buried immediately after they died, but a family might have to wait for months to experience the consolation of a religious service. This was especially true if the loved one passed away in the late fall or winter when roads were impassable. There are some cited instances where a funeral took place *decades* after the deceased had passed.

In the rugged mountains, where a speedy remarriage for a bereaved spouse was sometimes crucial for survival, it wasn't uncommon for a widow or widower to attend the funeral of their *late* spouse with their *new* spouse on their arm. Funeralizing also meant that services were sometimes conducted in bulk, with a circuit preacher performing funerals, along with weddings and baptisms, for several members of a community at once. It was not unheard of to even conduct a funeral *prior* to a person dying, if a good circuit preacher was around, and death—and cold weather—seemed imminent.[4]

Funerals were therefore a significant event in the life of a mountain town. Family and friends would come from miles around and the entire community was involved. Massive amounts of food were prepared, and because the grieved had had some amount of time to absorb the loss, the occasion took on a festive and celebratory mood. Fall was an ideal time for a funeral because the weather was still decent and the work of the year's harvest had been completed. Grave sites, some of which had been dug a year earlier, were cleared and cleaned up before the funeral took place.

This ritual of cleaning and preparing grave sites may have been the precursor to Decoration Day in Appalachia.[5] Different churches and communities had different days designated as their own Decoration Day, but typically the event would take place on a Sunday during late spring, summer, or early fall. The Saturday before Decoration Day would be spent cleaning all the graves in the cemetery. Sunday, the day the actual decoration would take place, was filled with music, singing, laughter, crying, food, and story-telling. Everyone would gather for a religious service with hymns, prayers, and preaching, and graves were decorated with flowers.

Originally, Appalachian cemeteries were clean dirt yards on hill-sides, and part of the Decoration event was to clear the weeds, grass, and saplings that had grown over the graves since the last Decoration Day. Gravestones were simple. Some were simply large, plain fieldstones, while others were carved by local craftsmen or neighbors who were handy with a chisel.[6] *Mounding* was the practice of putting fresh dirt and sand over a grave where the earth had settled or sunken in. Mounding would continue as a ritual of Decoration Day long after the grave required it because for many, it felt like a reenactment of the original burial. Mounds, decorated as they often were with a single row of flowers, reflected the imagery of a typical Appalachian vegetable garden, a symbol of new life.[7]

Most people today who still practice Decoration Day use store-bought plastic flowers to adorn graves. These durable flourishes are slow to fade and will often maintain their pop of color even through the long winter months. In years past, people collected real flowers—"ivy" (mountain laurel) and "red laurel" (red rhododendron) and any wildflower that was in bloom.[8] It was also customary to make flowers out of crepe paper to place on the graves. Some families would spend the entire winter folding delicate paper blossoms of various colors and then store them in cardboard boxes until Decoration Day arrived.[9]

Older generations remember Decoration Day as being one of

the most significant holidays of the year. People would wear their best clothes and prepare the best recipes. For families who traveled from far and wide, it was a time to reconnect and share memories. It was even a time for young people, dressed up in the latest fashions, to scout for marriage prospects.[10]

A Decoration Day service would take place at or very near the cemetery. A preacher would facilitate the service and there was always a choir or musical group that would lead in the singing of the old mountain hymns. The service would reach its emotional peak as people began to recount remembrances and testimonials of their lost loved ones. Tears were shed and laughter was shared.[11]

"Dinner on the grounds" is a term used for the potluck meal served picnic-style in the church yard or cemetery at the Decoration Day service. Almost like a graveyard Communion service, dinner on the grounds would involve the fellowship of the saints, plus buttermilk biscuits, fried chicken, corn bread, berry pies, and apple stack cakes.

Sadly, as the years have gone by, the customs surrounding Decoration Day have started to fade from the Appalachian countryside. Families have moved and old cemeteries remain unvisited and unkempt. Or landscaping companies with no tie to the cemetery are paid to mow it a few times a year. There are still churches that maintain some of the traditions. You can always tell which ones those are. You might be driving through the mountains on a sunny afternoon, the hillsides heavy with the green growth of late summer. Suddenly, there is a clearing and a vibrant splash of color—red, pink, yellow, blue, and white plastic flowers piled on top of headstones and arranged in neat rows across graves.

Almost every year since I moved to the mountains ten years ago, my aunt has asked me if I wanted to come to Decoration Day at the old family cemetery in Bakersville. In years past, I honestly didn't fully understand what she was asking me to attend. I'd always ignore the call or text, or I'd come up with some excuse for why I couldn't make the hour-long drive over there.

This year, however, I was eagerly awaiting my invitation to Decoration Day at the Burleson Family Cemetery. I had visions of picnic tables filled with fried okra, sliced homegrown tomatoes, peach cobblers, and deviled eggs. I pictured myself reconnecting with second cousins and great-aunts I hadn't seen since I was a little girl, and I imagined raising our voices together, singing the old songs and sharing fond memories.

But when I asked my aunt about Decoration Day this year, she said, "Oh, they don't really do that anymore. At least not like they used to." There is no service or singing. There is no picnic. Families still decorate the graves of their relations on the first weekend in September. But they do it on their own time and don't make a big show about it.

I missed it. A ritual passed away before my very eyes. I'd been too busy, too caught up in the demands of life. *I* had participated in its extinction.

• • • • •

One fascinating aspect of Decoration Day is how the tradition traveled, in limited but profound ways. The practice of Decoration Day can be found in small pockets across the Upland South, extending into Arkansas and Texas. There are even areas of Ontario, Canada, that observe Decoration Day.[12]

Decoration Day is also widely practiced in Liberia, the West African nation originally established as a colony of the United

States to "return" and "repatriate" free people of color back to Africa beginning in 1822. In fact, Decoration Day as a cultural practice is much more intact in Liberia than it is in Appalachia. In Liberia, it is a national holiday, recognized annually on the second Wednesday in March. The whole country shuts down for Decoration Day as families gather at cemeteries to clean grave sites, eat food, and share memories.

I spoke with my Liberian friend Gentry about Decoration Day in his country recently. Like many Liberian holidays, he tells me Decoration Day was borrowed from American traditions, a ritual hand-me-down that has been repurposed and reimagined to serve the needs of the Liberian people within their context. It likely journeyed across the ocean with emancipated slaves and free people of color who had lived and labored in the Upland South. As with many other aspects of Liberian culture, the American practice was interwoven with traditional tribal customs. Overt expressions of communion with the dead are of particular importance in parts of West Africa. At Decoration Day celebrations in Liberia, it is not uncommon to see libations offered to the deceased, with alcoholic beverages poured over the graves.

Gentry told me that Decoration Day practices vary from region to region and family to family. In many cemetery gatherings, the occasion takes on a very somber tone, with people wailing over the graves and memorializing lost loved ones. Graves are scrubbed clean and sometimes painted. In recent years, Decoration Day has developed into a more festive atmosphere. He tells me the younger generation of Liberians treat Decoration Day as an excuse to party—a time to eat, drink, and celebrate.

To this day, Liberians are still reckoning with what it means to be a nation whose social fabric is made up of the descendants of former slaves, colonizers, African Americans, and West Africans of various tribal groups. Decoration Day recognizes the impact of these ancestors and honors the legacy they have left behind.

But something Gentry told me got me thinking that Decoration Day does more than simply honor the lives of the deceased. He told me that traditional tribal beliefs emphasize the ongoing role that the dead play in our lives. That is why many people, particularly on Decoration Day, will take time to talk to the dead. People will weep aloud and report to the dead loved one all the important events that have transpired since their passing: births, marriages, hardships, employment lost or found, natural disasters, hunger or plenty.

On Decoration Day, it seems, we tell the stories of our loved ones. And we tell our own stories. We recognize the impact the loss has had on us, and the way we have journeyed forward. In Appalachia and Liberia, on Decoration Day, we gather with the community of the living. Standing over the bodily remains of our lost loved ones, we commemorate what remains above—the love we continue to share for them and for one another, the character they shaped, the lives they helped build, the way the human spirit triumphs over tragedy.

Many people think that grief is primarily the endeavor to honor the memory of the deceased. To grieve well is to deflect, to minimize our own experiences in the name of elevating the stories of our lost loved ones. We marinate in our survivor's guilt. We feel the competing sweetness and shame of the privilege of living. *I must become small*, we may think to ourselves, *so that the dead do not disappear.*

But survival is not a zero-sum game. To belittle our own existence in the name of another dishonors the image of God in us and His sovereign choice to allow us to go on living. Many of the beautiful rituals of grief I've studied are as much about honoring our own experience of loss as they are about honoring the lives of the dead. A ritual holds space for both purposes. And perhaps that's how it should be.

• • • • •

Why do I get to go on living?

It's a question I've asked myself a million times. What makes me more deserving than the dead? And what do I do with myself now that I am walking around with this horrible wound and deep sense of knowing what it means to be mortal?

What has been accomplished by all this grief? Is there any silver lining, any redemption to be found? Is the wisdom I've gained worth the loss I've endured? Wouldn't I still go back and change it all? Wouldn't I beckon my babies' hearts to keep beating and beg my sister to find a way to stay? Wouldn't I trade all the lessons learned to have them back?

Two and a half years after my sister's death and a year and a half after my last miscarriage, I still find myself in worship services feeling so wary, so numb, so cynical. I confess there have even been a few times that I considered walking away from the faith altogether. I was trying to connect with the Lord in prayer, in worship, through the reading of the Word, but somehow, my soul still felt like an empty cavern.

For years, I've taught aid workers that it's best not to make major life decisions in the immediate aftermath of a traumatic event. With that admonition in mind, when it came to my faith in God, I decided not to decide. I decided to wait, to watch, to pray. I decided to be patient, to not come to any conclusions, at least not right away.

I'm not going to tell you that God showed up in an undeniable way. I'm not going to say He spoke audibly to me in the whirlwind or even in the silence. I'm not going to tell you He appeared in a vision or gave me signs and wonders.

But something happened inside me in the midst of my grief that I cannot deny. I was being shaped, molded. I was growing in wisdom, in compassion, in patience, and in strength. Yes, this new growth was running parallel to my increased anxiety, sadness, and anger. But somehow, somewhere, the beauty of God's work in my life seemed to overtake the ugliness of it all, eclipsed it in some mysterious way.

That eclipsing was the miracle I had trouble squaring with the atheistic worldview I was dabbling in. God *must* have been real. I didn't exactly feel God making my life easier, assuaging all my fears, or alleviating all my sadness. But I did feel Him molding me. I felt Him guiding me. I didn't like it at first, and there are certainly still times that I miss the old me. I can't explain it, but His tutelage of me in this season has been one of the most powerful and intimate experiences of my life.

In 2 Corinthians chapter 1, Paul shares about some of the struggles he and his companions experienced in ministry, struggles so discouraging that he "felt we had received the sentence of death" (v. 9). But in verses prior to this, he praises God, who is the Father of compassion, who is able to comfort us. When we receive this comfort, we then, in turn, are able to comfort others.

This passage may be one of the most frequently quoted bits of Scripture as a response to grief. I confess, I've always had mixed feelings about these verses. There were plenty of days where I did not experience the *feeling* of comfort. And I wondered if God had failed in His promise. Or perhaps I had failed somehow in accessing the goodness of God.

Biblical commentator John Short has this to say about the inadequacy of the translation of the word "comfort" (*parakalon*): "Comfort is a word which in modern speech has lost much of its [New Testament] meaning. It suggests to us a kind of sedative, a palliative for pain of body or mind. But the comfort of God is no narcotic." He goes on to say that the word for "comforter," when applied to the Holy Spirit, actually means "strengthener." It's the same root from which we get the word "fortify." "We comfort a sufferer," he writes, "when we give him courage to bear his pain or face his misfortune. Comfort is what sets him on his feet."[13]

Grief gave birth to something in me. I can't even name it. I can't describe it. It is a very particular and mysterious form of strength that is both humbled and emboldened. I wouldn't wish those labor pains on anyone. But I cherish the outcome. "Let perseverance finish its work so that you may be mature and complete, not lacking anything" (James 1:4).

I don't in any way think of myself as "complete." I've noticed that many self-help books, including grief-oriented self-help books, tend to be written by folks who have developed a sense of confidence in their own ability to overcome their challenges. They peddle that confidence to hurting consumers and insist that everyone apply the same blueprint that worked for them.

Let me be clear. I have not figured this out. I'm still fumbling my way through grief. I've numbed, I've stubbornly refused to ask for help, I've thrown things, I've pretended to be fine, I've isolated, I've almost given up.

And...

God has been here. As my boss said, God has helped me. If comfort is a good feeling, then God failed. But if comfort is fortification, then God has more than made good on His promise.

If I could offer one word of advice about grief, I would say this: Stay. Stay on the path. Lean into the elements. Carry the load and don't put it down. Endure. You *will* reap a harvest. God will help you.

I will never say that my grief has been good. But I will say that it has not been wasted. Not one bit. As I wrote in the beginning, sometimes you must let grief have its way with you. Resist the urge to deny or numb. Rather, remain under the brutal burden of grief. Stare it straight in the eye. Somehow, some way, grief has made me who I am today. The sorrow that threatened to break me apart is now the cement that holds me together.

• • • • •

Recently, a reporter came to my hometown to interview my family and a handful of my sister's friends about her impact in the world and in our lives. We stayed up late into the night, talking on my brother-in-law's back porch, sharing stories about growing up with Rachel, how she'd found her voice in her high school and college years, how she'd grown into the indomitable force that she was within American Christian culture.

But while Rachel was the unifying thread in each of our anecdotes, the stories we shared were as much about us and our own journeys as they were about Rachel. They were stories of faith lost and found, of character formed and fashioned, of love and compassion purified in the refining fire of grief. They were stories of triumph over tribulation, of finding joy amid the sorrow, of how *her* life and love had shaped *our* lives. It was a sacred night. A hard night. A good night.

More than a postmortem photograph, more than a decorated headstone, more than a memento mori necklace, and more than a wail or the resounding toll of a bell, Rachel's life echoes on in the world through the faithful and brave living on of the people whose lives she changed. Her heart beats on in the hearts of those who have been changed by her love for us and our love for her. By telling our own stories, we tell *her* story.

Death will not steal from me the blessing of what it was to know and love Rachel and call her my very own sister. It cannot rob me of the joy of having had her in my life. To be grateful for her despite the pain of her loss is an act of resistance, a declaration that I will not be defeated by the tyranny of death.

Frankly, there is no epitaph, no monument, no memorial that could adequately convey all that my sister is and was. Even the most attentive, ardent stewardship of her memory will never bring her back. But I am here. We are here. We are the living stones that testify to her life and impact. Our lives are her memorial. By honoring ourselves, we honor her.

• • • • •

The first Sunday of September is Decoration Day at the Burleson Family Cemetery in Bakersville, North Carolina. No, it is not the large celebration it once was. There is no potluck or hymn singing. But families do still come at some point in the weekend and lay flowers on the graves of loved ones. I drove over there the Monday after Decoration Day, this time with little Lois, who was six months old at the time.

The day was bright, and the beating sun drew a sweat despite the chill of the coming autumn in the breeze. As I turned my Subaru onto the backroad leading to the cemetery, I noticed that this time, the heavy, rusted gate was swung open. Lois had been lulled to sleep as we traversed the winding mountain roads, so after I parked my car under the trees, I cracked the windows, turned the car off, and left her dreaming in the backseat.

I walked onto the neatly mowed cemetery knoll. I'd come prepared. The week before I'd spent almost an hour in the floral section of the local craft store, meticulously searching for just the right arrangements. I tried to remember what my grandmother's favorite flower was, which colors my grandfather liked the best. In the end, I went with some bright black-eyed Susans and white daisies on the sale rack. Plastic flowers, it turns out, are pretty pricey.

As my eyes adjusted to the glaring sunlight, I could see that sure enough, the grassy knoll was covered in bright flowers of every color. The leaves were raked and the branches cleared. The fence was repaired, and the stones were clean. Some grave markers were more elaborately decorated. One had at least a dozen stems sticking up out of the ground around the stone. Others had been adorned with flags and crosses.

Most astonishingly, every single grave had a single, fresh-cut pink hydrangea blossom on it—*every single grave*, whether it had a brand-new stone or one 150 years old; whether it was an infant who died the day she was born or an old man who lived into his nineties; whether it had a large headstone with an intricate carving, a simple wooden cross, or a century-old fieldstone half buried and long forgotten.

I'm not sure who put the hydrangeas there. Because I've never been to Decoration Day, I'm not sure if it is an annual tradition at the Burleson Cemetery, or if someone had simply had a particularly prolific hydrangea bush that year. Nevertheless, it was a tender and reverent offering.

I carried my flowers over to my grandparents' graves and arranged them in a way I liked. I wandered through the cemetery with a watchful eye on my Subaru where Lois was still sleeping. I found the grave of a distant cousin and an infant child of his I never knew existed. I found the graves of my great-great-great-grandfather and -grandmother and left a flower for them.

"We are okay," I told them. "We made it. We survived. I just thought you should know. And Lois is here. You should see her. She has the best smile."

● ● ● ● ●

I drove to the family graveyard by way of Carver's Gap, a high mountain pass near the top of the Roan. There is a narrow highway that cuts through the pass and if you turn at Carver's Gap to the west, a road takes you up to Roan High Knob and the rhododendron gardens. If you park instead at Carver's Gap, you can connect by foot to the portion of the Appalachian Trail that traverses the balds of the Roan Highlands: Round Bald, Grassy Ridge Bald, and Jane's Bald.

Growing up, I'd always heard from the locals that Jane's Bald was named for a woman who had died of milk poisoning while crossing the mountain sometime back in the 1800s. I didn't know what milk poisoning was exactly, but I always felt a chill run down my spine when we'd ascend that part of the mountain and approach the crude wooden sign marking the top of Jane's Bald.

It turns out that this popular synopsis, though prevalent, is not the complete story. The story of Jane's Bald is a story of a family of sisters. Appalachian journalist Michael Joslin interviewed Elsie Yelton, the granddaughter of the woman who actually died. He published her account in 1999 in the *Johnson City Press*.[14]

According to Elsie, in 1870 her grandmother Harriett decided to cross the Roan from North Carolina with her sister Jane in order to visit their two other sisters who lived on the Tennessee side of the mountain. Harriett had recently recovered from milk poisoning, a disease brought on by drinking milk from a cow that had eaten the white snakeroot plant. She felt she was strong enough to make the journey, though another sister, Judy, warned her and Jane not to go. After an uneventful crossing and a good visit with the Tennessee sisters, Jane and Harriett began their return trek home over the Roan on November 16.

The weather shifted, as it is apt to do in the mountains, from warm and sunny to cold and cloudy. Harriett became weaker and weaker as they climbed higher and higher, and by the time they reached the balds, the milk sickness had returned and made her extremely ill. Unable to continue on, Harriett and Jane hunkered down on the mountain for the night, the wind whipping around them. Jane didn't leave her sister's side, keeping vigil over her weakening body, watching for bears and bobcats.

At first light, Jane fled down the mountain in search of help. Charley Young, who lived in a cabin not far from Carver's Gap, brought his wagon as far as he could, then climbed up to find Harriett still alive, but very frail. He helped both women into the wagon. Jane was almost frozen to death herself. Harriett, who was only twenty-four, died shortly after they finally made it home.

Jane, however, went on to live a long life well into the 1940s. No doubt she carried the memory of that fateful journey always.

From the day of Harriett's death onward, all the locals called that portion of the mountain Jane's Bald, in honor of the fierce, freezing vigil Jane kept at her sister's side. In honor of her pain. In honor of her loss.

That Monday after Decoration Day, I parked my car at Carver's Gap. I strapped Lois to my chest and began to climb. As always, there is a world of weather at the top of the mountain. But this time, it was different. This time, the heavy mist occasionally parted, and the sun peeked through. I stood on the mossy trail, Lois breathing on my neck. If I waited long enough, I could see the swirling fog reveal the valley below, hillsides and hollows stretching a million miles in every direction.

Up on these balds, my heart ached for Jane. At one point in our hike, the trail parted and I began to fear I'd gone the wrong way. In the heavy mist without the benefit of a horizon, it's easy to get lost, to lose your sense of east and west, of up from down. She must have been so scared up there on that bald in the dark, cold unknown. Waiting for the sun to rise. Waiting for the first glimpse of light.

But this was not my first time on the Roan. It wouldn't be my last. Lois and I made our way on the well-worn path and soaked in the highlands until her tiny whimper told me she was hungry and it was time to go home. I took one last look at the bald. Mountains are absorbent, as Annie Dillard said. This mountain held pain. It held loss. It held hope. It held memory, my memories. "Look, Amanda! I'm flying! I'm flying through the clouds!"

Jane. Harriett. Two sisters. And a mountain, named not in honor of the one who died, but in honor of the one who lived. The one who grieved.

Afterword

Faith and grief. They make strange bedfellows. And yet they are more akin than one would think. Both are lifelong journeys. Both are intrinsic to the human experience. Both can feel like they blind you and open your eyes in one swift motion. Both are at times mother, father, tutor, taskmaster, and tyrant.

"It's not a religion! It's a relationship!" As an evangelical in America, I heard this a lot growing up. In this season of grief, I've found that my *relationship* with God did not always help. But my *religion* did.

Let me explain what I mean.

My rapport with God during the last few years has felt a bit like a tumultuous high school dating relationship. If Jesus was my "boyfriend"—as so many mantras of the purity movement told me—He didn't always seem like a very good one. He'd disappointed me, upended my life, made promises He didn't seem to keep, and at times felt absent. We were *not* emotionally connecting. I realize this was simply my perception of Him as I worked through my losses. Still, it wasn't the heartwarming, fulfilling, ardent relationship I'd come to expect from the lover God.

At some point, I stopped relying on the warm and fuzzy

emotional support of a one-on-one relationship with God, and instead turned to religion. By this I mean that I turned to communal liturgy. I turned to scripted confessions of the faith. I repeated affirmations of historic doctrine. Much like my sister, I clung to the rituals and ancient traditions of the church. I committed to a faith that was more of a shared endeavor than an individual feeling. I observed noteworthy days on the church calendar. I had ash smeared on my forehead for Lent. I feasted on Easter. I lit candles for Advent and ate king cake for Epiphany. I read the daily offices and folded my hands for prayer at meals. Every day, I took another step. I didn't always expect God to "show up." But I made a commitment that I would show up for the liturgy of life with God.

I did the same with grief. I didn't know what to say, what to think, or what to feel. My mind was all over the place; my heart was shattered. So I set my body in motion.

I put on black clothing. I ate casseroles that people delivered. I tore open sealed envelopes and read pastel-colored sympathy cards, taking in every word. I'd go sit in my car and scream. I wandered through cemeteries. I looked through old photographs. I decorated graves with plastic flowers.

What I found in rooting myself in a long history of bodily and spiritual movements around grief was that ritual creates a placeholder for emotion. I did not have to perform or make things up as I went along. A path had been carved for me by millions of saints and mourners in the past. I could walk in their footsteps until I found my own footing. I was handed a script, a communal habit that mourners and condolers alike have shared as they walked together. No one knows how to act or what to say when faced with the atrocity of death. Rituals tell us what to say. They tell us how to act. They give us another step.

Psychologists note that some form of avoidance is natural and even healthy in the immediate aftermath of loss. Evasion helps us regulate the disabling and chaotic emotional experience of fresh grief. The bereaved tend to oscillate between two responses: the inclination to repress the pain, and the inclination to expose oneself to the death and the agony of the loss.[1] This oscillation is normal and to some degree may even help us survive.

My experience is that rituals introduce a healthy rhythm of exposure to the grief. They allow us to let off emotional steam at specific moments. With a ritual, you willingly confront your losses head-on a few times a day or a few times a week, so that you don't have to be beholden to them all the time. Rituals name and order the chaos of our emotions.

Rituals invite the community into our space of sorrow. They provide actions, services, and words for use by others who want to help but might not know how. They alleviate awkwardness, naming and embracing the elephant in the room. Rituals create communal choreography and synchronize our sorrow.

A sturdy, time-honored ritual is pliant and adaptable. I made some rituals my own, repurposed them to fit the moment. These secondhand sacraments grow in beauty as they are handed down again and again. We each add our stitches to the holes, add brushes of color to what has faded.

The truth is, grief requires presence so much more than it requires perfection or performance. The same is true of faith. All I had to do was show up for the ritual and then grief began to transform me all on its own in important and beautiful ways. That's often how faith works too. By showing up for liturgy and tradition, I found that God had been there all along. The habits themselves were healing. My heart and my body just needed to catch up with the truth. Even when I didn't feel it, God was with me. He was for-tifying me. He was giving me wisdom and grace for the challenges. Together, we shared the labor of grief. And we shared the labor of faith.

• • • • •

A few weeks before Lois was born, I was talking with my friend Sarah about my aches and pains and how ready I was to go into labor and birth this child. As she always does, Sarah spoke peace over me: "Be patient, lass. Her last threads are being woven." (Sarah is Scottish, so her words always have a sage, melodic quality to them.)

She then said something I'll never forget. She explained that in her mind, the birth of my daughter was the first step in a long jour-ney of releasing this soul that was knit in me—that was truly a part of me—into the world. It's a de-possessing of her. It's an acceptance that we are *not* one, that she is wholly other than me, and that her path will take her incrementally further and further away from me. Birthing is the labor of letting go and accepting the possibility that she may come to a point someday where she is no more.

I guess love always creates a liminal space, between discovering and losing, between joy and sadness, between embracing and releas-ing. Birth is always the beginning of death. From the moment my daughter comes wailing from my womb, she will begin the process of dying. The question is, am I willing to learn to love her in this new way, in a way that names the potential of loss, of undoing—the unraveling of all those threads? Am I willing to entrust her to the One who conceived of her from the beginning?

The One who gives and takes away. The One who takes away

and gives. The One whose name is blessed and whose name I bless with every kiss, every embrace, every moment of laughter, every second of savoring.

• • • • •

I suppose someday I may regret writing a book about bereavement only two to three years after my most significant losses. I have not yet matured into my grief, have probably not arrived at the redeeming vantage point I pray is in the future. Time does not heal all wounds. But it does bring wisdom. It illuminates lessons.

The advantage, perhaps, of writing this book now, though, is that I only have the vocabulary for fresh sorrow. Confounding pain is still the language I know best and maybe, if you've picked up this book, that is the only language you can comprehend right now, too. And so, we understand one another. At least, I hope we do.

I am not a historian. I am not an anthropologist. I am not a psychologist. And I'm not a theologian. I am just a person who has experienced loss. I have felt grief deeply. I was unprepared. Also, I survived.

I've learned a lot about history, anthropology, psychology, and theology by reading about grief rituals. I've also learned a lot about myself. I wouldn't think so highly of myself to offer a comprehensive analysis of where we are as a society when it comes to our grief. Any recommendations I make would only be partially informed and certainly subjective.

In the writing of this book, I've realized how easy it is to feel nostalgic about the past. The strict structures of the Victorian period warn us against being overly sentimental. There was no one era that got things exactly right, no generation that was completely adept at managing our mortality. So there is no reason to think that this current generation is incapable of instituting healthy communal rituals. We have much to learn from our past, imperfect though it may be. And we have much to learn from other cultures around the world that still maintain a robust array of historic rituals, traditions I didn't attempt to fully explore in this book for fear of misrepresenting or unfairly appropriating.

I am afraid as a Western, American culture that we are not moving in the right direction. I am concerned about the impact COVID-19 has had on our grief rituals. As we have seen, large-scale catastrophic events sometimes create irreversible shifts in the way we grieve. The Black Plague of the 1300s weakened the regularity and uniformity of death rituals across Europe. Outbreaks of smallpox and yellow fever turned public opinion against the practice of tolling the bell. The Civil War instigated the outsourcing of bodily burial preparations. World War I put a stop to the wearing of mourning clothes out of fear the public would be demoralized.

My friend Sargon tells me that in the Iraqi village where he grew up, it was customary for the community to forgo Christmas or Easter celebrations if someone from the village had recently passed away. This was their way of honoring the dead and the family who was in grief. Sargon says that when he was a young man and the war started, the village went for years without celebrating the holidays because so many people were dying. Death was constant. They were losing one sacred ritual in the name of another. Sargon tells me after five or six years, people gave up and began celebrating the holidays again in spite of the losses because it just wasn't practical to carry on the tradition.

Some rituals shift for good reasons. But some are lost without any thought toward tending to the emotional need that was *beneath* the practice. What rituals will this pandemic steal from us? The prohibition of large funeral gatherings for the sake of public health won't last forever. When we are once again allowed to gather to mourn together, will we? Or will we see it as unnecessary, an outdated custom? Will we see it as an inconvenience, a demoralizing detour from our toxically positive paths of self-actualization?

Rituals have much to offer us. Keening affirms our anguish. Covering mirrors gives us grace for the change. Telling the bees invites peace and courage into the precarity. Shivah intrudes upon our loneliness with presence. Casseroles bring us back into our bodies. Photographs help us remember rightly. Sympathy cards give us words to express our love. Wearing black allows us to be honest about what we are feeling on the inside. Tolling the bell summons us to accept the everlasting burden of grief. Funeral games make space for joy. Death rooms remind us of our mortality. Decoration Day honors our loved ones and our own stories.

It is my personal belief that rituals are most powerful when practiced in community. We all have our own daily habits, personal practices that soothe or strengthen us. As I've studied historic traditions of grief, I've done my best to begin implementing rituals that spoke to me, that made sense for my day-to-day. But for the most part, I have practiced these alone.

How do you convince an entire society to return to or reinvent a long-forgotten tradition? How do we pull people away from the idol of individualism, the enticing efficiency of technology, and the palliative comfort of entertainment long enough to convince them that the slow, intentional presence of a communal ritual is good and healthy for us all?

One thing I can't decide is this: Is the church a preserver of rituals or a destroyer of rituals? I've seen many instances where a theological discrepancy or power struggle has led to the church snuffing out a grief tradition with no obvious attempt to replace it. And yet, the church is also the keeper of many rituals of lament, repentance, and remembrance. Ours is the church of All Saints' Day and All Souls' Day. Ours is the church of Ash Wednesday and Communion. The church ritualizes the longing of Advent and holds space for the loss of the holy innocents even amid the Christmas season. The church embraces the sorrow of the cross! And the church is still the place many of us chose to go to marry, to bury, and to baptize. A pastor or priest is still often the person we want presiding over these ceremonies.

As much as I've criticized the church's historic wariness of some of these rituals, I actually believe that the church is uniquely positioned to lead society to this end. The church is one of the few remaining communal institutions that is still intact. And the holy Scriptures of the church, the Word of God, is full of raw and relatable truth about the experience of grief and sorrow, so much more than I ever anticipated. Most powerful of all, the God we worship is a God who chose to descend into the depths of our grief so He could rescue us from sin and pain forever. His empathy, His identification as a mourner, and His surrender to death *was His glory*. His triumph. And we share in that glory, that triumph.

What if the church invited society back into grief? Back to traditions, back to rituals, back to communal ceremonies of sorrow. What if our church buildings were places where the whole spectrum of human emotions was not only recognized but indulged, tended to, shepherded, surrounded by community, and supported with holy habits?

At the very least, I would ask that we not be lazy, that we not lose our remaining rituals due to neglect or distraction. Let's not move quickly along as we do with so many of our hurts and discomforts these days. Could we creatively engage and discern together new ways to move our bodies into the motions of grief? Could we be fully present in our bodies? Could we write new scripts for sharing condolence and offering one another comfort? Could we rediscover rituals for our own time, our own place? Could we try it together?

• • • • •

It is Ash Wednesday, 2021. The pandemic is not over. But my parents have just been vaccinated. And I am just two weeks away from giving birth to little Lois.

Many churches have not begun meeting regularly for services yet, and some that had relaunched Sunday gatherings over the summer decided to scale back again during the surge of cases over the holidays. We are in the dark days of this crisis, with the daily death rate reaching the thousands in our country alone.

But I am determined to observe Ash Wednesday in honor of my sister and in honor of the griefs I've borne in the last few years. I feel the nearness of labor in my aching hips. I am scared. I am excited. I am uncertain. I need to remind myself that I am mortal and that's okay. I need to wear the humbling smear of ashes on my face. I need to be told I am dust and to dust I will return.

This year, I pull into the parking lot of St. Luke's on time. But just barely. I couldn't find a clear answer on the church's website about whether or not they'd be holding a service in person. I brought my mask and was prepared to socially distance in the sanctuary.

Once again, I have trouble finding the entrance. I'm not sure what it is about the design of this building, but I just can't seem to ever find my way inside. The weather is warm considering it is February in Boone, so I walk the perimeter of the church a couple of times looking for an unlocked door. Actually, I'm waddling. And cursing myself for wearing wedge shoes when I am nine months pregnant.

The rector must have seen me passing by the window a few times. She comes to the side door, puts on her mask, and greets me. I ask her if they are having the noon service and she says no, but that if I email the church secretary, I can get a Zoom link for future services. I assure her that I understand and thank her. She blesses me and sends me on my way.

Rather than going back to my car, I wander around for a bit on the grounds of the church. There is a small prayer chapel that is also locked. And there is a prayer labyrinth, a circular maze of flat stones leading to a Celtic cross at the center. As the sun warms my sore back, I decide to walk the maze slowly, and pray. COVID has once again upended a treasured ritual. So I have to get creative.

Many of the stones have been inscribed and are dedicated to the memory of lost loved ones. I read their names carefully as I pass, sometimes praying for their families, wondering what their lives had been like. I move slowly in the circle of the maze, each orbit getting smaller and smaller, moving me closer and closer to the cross. It reminds me of a poem from one of my sister's favorite poets, Rainer Maria Rilke:

> *I live my life in widening circles*
> *That reach out across the world.*
> *I may not complete this last one*
> *but I give myself to it.*[2]

Around and around. Ashes to ashes. I feel myself coming uncoiled with every step. Dust to dust. "Stay on the path, Amanda." I begin to cry.

The poem continues:

> *I circle around God, around the primordial tower.*
> *I've been circling for thousands of years*
> *and I still don't know: am I a falcon,*
> *a storm, or a great song?*[3]

Sometimes I feel like I am always circling grief—a dark, endless hole that threatens to pull me into its void. What keeps me from falling in? Fear? Courage? Hope? God Himself?

But today, on Ash Wednesday, I am circling the cross, that fierce instrument of death that bought me life. The tears I am crying today are not just tears of sadness. They are tears of joy too. "Thank You, God." My baby kicks my ribs. Another step. "Thank You, God." My only sister is gone. "Why, Lord? I will *never* understand." Another step. I remember that I am dust, and to dust I will return. "Won't you spare me over 'til another year?" The sun shines on my face. Another step. "Thank You, God." Another step. "Help my baby to live." Another step. "Make me glad for as many days as I've seen trouble."

These are my prayers this Ash Wednesday. To the God who gives. And takes away. And gives. Another step.

Acknowledgments

I am so grateful to my agent, Rachelle Gardner, for your faith in me and my writing. Thank you for all the ways you've supported me both professionally and personally in the last three years. This book would not exist without you.

Thank you to my editor, Beth Adams, Daisy Hutton, and all the good folks at Hachette and Worthy Publishing for believing in this project and your tireless efforts to bring it to the world.

To our community here in Boone, there aren't words to express how deeply grateful I am for the way you've carried us through our grief.

To my colleagues at Samaritan's Purse—your perseverance, courage, and tenderness in the face of suffering are an inspiration to every page in this book. Being your teammate was the honor of a lifetime.

I'm endlessly thankful to my Music Night crew. I'm blessed to be surrounded by such authentic, hardworking, creative people here in the mountains, including Erin Banks, John Lucas, Nicole Tester, Glenn and Erin Deuel, and Caroline and Everett Hardin. Sarah and Kevin DeShields, I'm thankful for all the creative work you poured into this project. Sarah, our campfire chats about birthing and dying and joy and sorrow are the reason this book exists.

Ethan Hardin, thank you so much for all the help you provided with the biblical research in this book. Your curiosity about the Scriptures pushed me deeper and added immensely to this project. And thanks to the entire community of theHeart Church in Boone. Seeking God together with you is a joy.

I'm thankful to Theresa Decker, Olivia Blinn, and Melissa Strickland for their wise advice on writing in the early stages of this project. Thank you, Joan Greene-Fisher, for your help researching sources. Thank you, Kelly Sites, for persistently praying for me as I wrote.

Thanks to Sophea West, Sargon Hormez, and Gentry Taylor for sharing so openly with me about grief rituals from your culture. Shelley Enarson, the day we had our conversation about shivah was the day this book took flight. Thank you.

My heartfelt gratitude to the Chaffes, Sarah Bessey, and Jeff Chu for all the kindness you have shown me in the form of cooking, knitting, talking, and praying.

I appreciate the good folks at the Watauga County Public Library and Appalachian State University Library for helping me find all the random, obscure, and creepy books I needed for research. Thanks also to Local Lion and Stickboy Kitchen for letting me park at a table with my laptop and write for hours.

Christin Bland, Joni Byker, Bev and Kendell Kauffeldt, Lizzy and Graham Aitken—I'm grateful for your enduring friendship.

To the entire Opelt family—thank you for loving me as your own daughter, granddaughter, and sister. Dennis and Jean, you were there for us when we needed you the most. Jean, your editorial eye, biblical wisdom, and enthusiasm for babysitting made it possible for me to finish this book in the way I wanted. Thank you.

I'm so grateful for the love of Dan, Jessie, and my niece and nephew, Harper and Henry. You've always been my biggest cheerleaders and I'm so proud of the bravery and compassion with which you've carried on.

Mom and Dad, you have shown me what it means to grieve with authenticity, courage, and grace. You tirelessly held me up in the midst of your own sorrow. I love you.

Sweet Jane—you brought us joy and light when we needed it the most. And you are a phenomenal sleeper. I wrote this book almost entirely during your afternoon naps. So perhaps you deserve more credit than anyone. Little Lois, you reminded us that love is always worth the risk. Somehow I believe you fought hard to exist, and I am so grateful to God that you did.

And to Tim. The world will never know the burdens you've carried, the secrets you've kept, the safe spaces you've guarded in this darkness. You are the night watchman and I'll love you forever.

Notes

Introduction: Ash Wednesday

1. The liturgy for this Ash Wednesday service was drawn from the Book of Common Prayer, 1979. which uses the New Revised Standard Version Bible: Anglicised Edition, copyright © 1989, 1995. The Psalter is from the Book of Common Prayer, 1979. https://www.bcponline.org/SpecialDays/ashwed.html.
2. Colin Dickey, "Behind the Draped Mirror," Hazlitt, accessed July 10, 2020, https://hazlitt.net/feature/behind-draped-mirror.

1: Keening (Anguish)

1. Annie Dillard, *Pilgrim at Tinker Creek* (New York: Quality Paperback Book Club ed., 1990), 3.
2. Suzanne E. Smith, *To Serve the Living: Funeral Directors and the African American Way of Death* (Cambridge, MA: Belknap Press of Harvard University Press, 2010), 22.
3. Sharon Blackie, "Mary McLaughlin," December 8, 2019, in *This Mythic Life*, https://sharonblackie.net/podcast/.
4. "Songs for the Dead," *BBC News World Service: Sounds*, March 15, 2017, https://www.bbc.co.uk/sounds/play/p04w50pq.
5. Clodagh Tait, *Death, Burial and Commemoration in Ireland, 1550–1650* (New York: Palgrave Macmillan, 2002), 36.
6. Blackie, "Mary McLaughlin."
7. Thomas H. Bestul, *Texts of the Passion: Latin Devotional Literature and Medieval Society* (Philadelphia: University of Pennsylvania Press, 1996), 171.
8. Andrea DenHoed, "Our Strange, Unsettled History of Mourning," *New Yorker*, February 3, 2016, https://www.newyorker.com/books/page-turner/our-strange-unsettled-history-of-mourning.
9. J. A. Thompson, *The Book of Jeremiah* (Grand Rapids, MI: William B. Eerdmans, 1980), accessed May 14, 2020, ProQuest Ebook Central.
10. William L. Holladay and Paul D. Hanson, *Jeremiah 1: A Commentary on the Books of the Prophet Jeremiah.* (Philadelphia: Fortress, 1986), Project MUSE, muse.jhu.edu/book/45965.
11. Juliana Claassens, *Mourner, Mother, Midwife: Reimagining God's Delivering Presence in the Old Testament* (Louisville: Westminster John Knox Press, 2012), e-book.

12. Claassens, *Mourner, Mother, Midwife.*

2: Covering Mirrors (Change)

1. Katy Kelleher, "The Ugly History of Beautiful Things," July 2019, *Longreads*, https://longreads.com/2019/07/11/the-ugly-history-of-beautiful-things-mirrors/.
2. Alessandra Pigni, *The Idealist's Survival Kit: 75 Simple Ways to Avoid Burnout* (Berkeley, CA: Parallax Press, 2016), 45.
3. Dylan Thomas, "Do not go gentle into that good night," in *The Poems of Dylan Thomas* (New York: New Directions, 1952, 1953), https://poets.org/poem/do-not -go-gentle-good-night.
4. Wayne D. Dosick, *Living Judaism: The Complete Guide to Jewish Belief, Tradition, and Practice* (New York: HarperOne, 1995), 309.
5. Jen Pollock Michel, *Surprised by Paradox: The Promise of "And" in an Either-Or World.* (Downers Grove, IL: InterVarsity Press, 2019), 161.
6. Zvi Ron, "Covering Mirrors in the Shiva Home," in *Hakirah* 13 (2012): 275, http://www.hakirah.org/Vol13Ron.pdf.
7. Sharon Blackie, *If Women Rose Rooted: A Life-Changing Journey to Authenticity and Belonging,* (September Publishing, 2016), 121–22.
8. Blackie, *If Women Rose Rooted,* 121–22.
9. Christopher Ash, *Job: The Wisdom of the Cross* (Wheaton, IL: Crossway, 2014), 53.
10. Ash, *Job,* 53.
11. Wendell Berry, *Hannah Coulter* (Washington: Shoemaker & Hoard, 2004), 57.
12. Dosick, *Living Judaism,* 309.
13. James K. Crissman, *Death and Dying in Central Appalachia: Changing Attitudes and Practices* (Chicago: University of Illinois Press, 1994), 25–26.
14. Rachel Held Evans, *A Year of Biblical Womanhood: How a Liberated Woman Found Herself Sitting on Her Roof, Covering Her Head, and Calling Her Husband Master* (Nashville: Thomas Nelson, 2016), 28.

3: Telling the Bees (Fear)

1. Hilda M. Ransome, *The Sacred Bee in Ancient Times and Folklore* (Mineola, NY: Dover, 2004), 221.
2. C. S. Lewis, *A Grief Observed* (London: Faber, 1961), 15.
3. "Life Expectancy," Centers for Disease Control and Prevention, National Center for Health Statistics, accessed August 24, 2021, https://www.cdc.gov/nchs/fastats/life -expectancy.htm.
4. Philippe Aries, *The Hour of Our Death: The Classic History of Western Attitudes Toward Death Over the Last One Thousand Years* (New York: Vintage Books, 2008), 586.
5. Brandy Schillace, *Death's Summer Coat: What the History of Death and Dying Can Tell Us About Life and Living* (New York: Pegasus Books, 2015), 79.
6. Norman F. Cantor, *In the Wake of the Plague: The Black Death and the World It Made* (New York: Free Press, 2001), 206.
7. Aries, *Hour of Our Death,* 116.
8. Aries, *Hour of Our Death,* 579-89.
9. John Greenleaf Whittier, "Telling the Bees," 1858. Poetry Foundation, accessed January 28, 2022, https://www.poetryfoundation.org/poems/45491/telling-the-bees.
10. Stephen Buchmann, *Letters from the Hive: An Intimate History of Bees, Honey, and Humankind* (New York: Bantam, 2006).

11. Richard Jones and Sharon Sweeney-Lynch, *The Beekeeper's Bible: Bees, Honey, Recipes, and Other Home Uses* (New York: Stewart, Tabori, and Chang, 2011), 12.

12. Colleen English, "Telling the Bees," *JStor Daily* (September 5, 2018), accessed August 21, 2021, https://daily.jstor.org/telling-the-bees/.

13. Steve Roud, *The Penguin Guide to the Superstitions of Britain and Ireland* (New York: Penguin, 2006).

14. Tammy Horn, *Bees in America: How the Honey Bee Shaped a Nation* (Lexington: University Press of Kentucky, 2005), 44.

15. Roud, *Penguin Guide*.

16. Ransome, *Sacred Bee*, 221.

17. Roud, *Penguin Guide*.

18. Mark Norman, *Telling the Bees and Other Customs: The Folklore of Rural Crafts* (Charleston, SC: History Press, 2020), 64.

19. Jan Richardson, *The Cure for Sorrow: A Book of Blessings for Times of Grief* (Orlando, FL: Wanton Gospeller Press, 2016), xviii.

20. Jones and Sweeney-Lynch, *Beekeeper's Bible*, 15–18.

21. Aaron O'Neill, "Childhood Mortality Rates (Under 5 Years Old) in the United States, 1800–2020," *Statista*, March 19, 2021, accessed August 24, 2021, https://www.statista.com/statistics/1041693/united-states-all-time-child-mortalityrate/#:~:text=%2C%20Mar%2019%2C%202021%20The%20child%20mortality%20rate,did%20not%20make%20it%20to%20their%20fifth%20birthday.

22. Daniel Taylor, *The Myth of Certainty: The Reflective Christian and the Risk of Commitment* (Downers Grove, IL: InterVarsity Press, 1986), 81.

4: Sitting Shivah (Presence)

1. Kate Bowler, *Everything Happens for a Reason: And Other Lies I've Loved* (New York: Random House, 2019), xiii–xiv.

2. Lisa Sharon Harper, *The Very Good Gospel: How Everything Wrong Can Be Made Right* (New York: WaterBrook, 2016), 13.

3. "Timeline of Jewish Mourning," accessed October 23, 2021, My Jewish Learning, https://www.myjewishlearning.com/article/timeline-of-jewish-mourning/.

4. Zalman Goldstein, "The Rules of Shiva," Chabad, accessed October 23, 2021, https://www.chabad.org/library/article_cdo/aid/370617/jewish/The-Rules-of-Shiva.htm.

5. Jessica Mitford, *The American Way of Death Revisited* (New York: Vintage Books, 1998), 52.

6. To find out more about Shelley Enarson and her incredible work, visit www.shelleyenarson.com.

7. "How Old Is the Kaddish?" Chabad, accessed October 23, 2021, https://www.chabad.org/library/article_cdo/aid/542330/jewish/How-Is-the-Kaddish.htm.

8. Dosick, *Living Judaism*, 307.

9. "Text of the Mourner's Kaddish," accessed October 23, 2021, My Jewish Learning, https://www.myjewishlearning.com/article/text-of-the-mourners-kaddish/.

10. Zalman Goldstein, "The Recitation of Kaddish," Chabad, accessed October 27, 2021, https://www.chabad.org/library/article_cdo/aid/371098/jewish/The-Recitation-of-Kaddish.htm.

11. Bowler, *Everything Happens for a Reason*, 121.

5: Casseroles (Body)

1. Dallas Willard, *Renovation of the Heart: Putting on the Character of Christ* (Colorado Springs: NavPress, 2002), 161.
2. Colin Murray Parkes and Holly G. Prigerson, *Bereavement: Studies of Grief in Adult Life* (New York: Routledge, 2010), 34–39.
3. Chris Raymond, "How to Cope with the Physical Effects of Grief," *Very Well Mind*, last modified March 24, 2020, accessed August 26, 2021, https://www.verywellmind.com/physical-symptoms-of-grief-4065135.
4. Thomas Buckley et al., "Physiological Correlates of Bereavement and the Impact of Bereavement Interventions." *Dialogues in Clinical Neuroscience* 14, no. 2 (2012): 129–39, doi:10.31887/DCNS.2012.14.2/tbuckley, https://www.ncbi.nlm.nih.gov/pmc/articles/PMC3384441/.
5. Aries, *Hour of Our Death*, 143.
6. Parkes and Prigerson, *Bereavement*, 15.
7. Aries, *Hour of Our Death*, 144.
8. Ralph, Houlbrooke, *Death, Religion, and the Family in England, 1480–1750* (Oxford: Clarendon Press, 1998), 223.
9. Maurice Lamm, "The Meal of Condolence in Judaism," Chabad, accessed October 23, 2021, https://www.chabad.org/library/article_cdo/aid/336479/jewish/The-Meal-of-Condolence-in-Judaism.htm.
10. Sarah Troop, "The Hungry Mourner," Modern Loss, July 2, 2014, accessed August 26, 2021, https://modernloss.com/food-death/.
11. Lisa Rogak, *Death Warmed Over: Funeral Food, Rituals, and Customs from Around the World* (Ten Speed Press, 2004), e-book.
12. Rogak, *Death Warmed Over*.
13. Hoag Levins, "The Story of Victorian Funeral Cookies: Revisiting a Centuries' Old Mourning Tradition," Historic Camden County, September 9, 2011, accessed September 9, 2021, http://historiccamdencounty.com/ccnews153.shtml.
14. Janet Reich Elsbach, *Extra Helping: Recipes for Caring, Connecting, and Building Community One Dish at a Time* (Boulder, CO: Roost Books, 2018), 120.
15. Bertram S. Puckle, *Funeral Customs: Their Origin and Development* (London: T. Werner Laurie, 1926), 104–7.
16. Rogak, *Death Warmed Over*.
17. Rogak, *Death Warmed Over*.
18. Rogak, *Death Warmed Over*.
19. Eva Selhub, "Nutritional Psychiatry: Your Brain on Food," *Harvard and Health Blog* 16, no. 11 (2015), https://www.health.harvard.edu/blog/nutritional-psychiatry-your-brain-on-food-201511168626.
20. Elsbach, *Extra Helping*, 1, 120.
21. Tish Harrison Warren, *The Liturgy of the Ordinary: Sacred Practices in Everyday Life* (Downers Grove, IL: InterVarsity Press, 2016), 63.

6: Postmortem Photography (Memory)

1. Schillace, *Death's Summer Coat*, 113.
2. Aaron O'Neill, "Life Expectancy (from Birth) in the United States from 1860 to 2020," *Statista*, February 3, 2021, https://www.statista.com/statistics/1040079/life-expectancy-united-states-all-time/.

3. Nancy West, "Pictures of Death," *Atlantic*, July 19, 2017, accessed August 26, 2021, https://www.theatlantic.com/technology/archive/2017/07/pictures-of-death/534060/.

4. Chris Woodyard, ed., *The Victorian Book of the Dead* (Dayton, OH: Kestrel, 2014), 155, 158.

5. Bethan Bell, *Taken from Life: The Unsettling Art of Death Photography*, BBC, June 5, 2016, accessed August 26, 2021, https://www.bbc.com/news/uk-england-36389581.

6. Mitch Albom, *Tuesdays with Morrie: An Old Man, a Young Man, and Life's Greatest Lesson* (New York City: Doubleday, 1997), 174.

7. Lewis, *Grief Observed*, 30.

8. Lewis, *Grief Observed*, 77–78.

9. Emily Dickinson, *The Complete Poems of Emily Dickinson* (Boston: Little, Brown, 1924); Bartleby.com, 2000, www.bartleby.com/113/.

10. N. T. Wright, *Surprised by Hope: Rethinking Heaven, the Resurrection, and the Mission of the Church* (New York: HarperOne, 2008), 36.

11. John Walton, *Old Testament Theology for Christians: From Ancient Context to Enduring Belief* (Downers Grove, IL: InterVarsity Press, 2017), 246.

12. Walton, *Old Testament Theology*, 239.

13. Marilynne Robinson, *Lila* (New York: Picador, 2014), 106.

14. Iris Gorfinkle, "It's Time to Stop Calling Pregnancy Loss Miscarriage," *Globe and Mail*, October 15, 2015, accessed August 26, 2021, https://www.theglobeandmail.com/life/health-and-fitness/health/its-time-to-stop-calling-pregnancy-loss miscarriage/article26823539/#:~:text=The%20term%20miscarriage%20is%20comprised,a%20%22means%20of%20conveyance.%22.

15. Jerry Sittser, *A Grace Disguised: How the Soul Grows through Loss* (Grand Rapids, MI: Zondervan, 1995), 99.

16. Susan Sontag, *On Photography* (New York: Picador, 1973), 15.

7: Sympathy Cards (Words)

1. Norman Melchert, *The Great Conversation: A Historical Introduction to Philosophy* (McGraw Hill, 2002), 605.

2. Michael Card, *A Sacred Sorrow: Reaching Out to God in the Lost Language of Lament* (Colorado Springs: NavPress, 2005), 21.

3. Ernest Dudley Chase, *The Romance of Greeting Cards: An Historical Account of the Origin, Evolution, and Development of the Christmas Card, Valentine, and Other Forms of Engraved or Printed Greetings* (Boston: University Press, 1926), 6 and 7.

4. "Sympathy: Product History," Hallmark, 2004, https://corporate.hallmark.com/holidays-occasions/sympathy/.

5. Schillace, *Death's Summer Coat*, 6–7.

6. Chase, *Romance of Greeting Cards*, 162–63.

7. Meghan O'Rourke, *The Long Goodbye: A Memoir* (New York: Riverhead Books, 2012).

8. Eric Schliesser, ed., *Sympathy: A History* (New York: Oxford University Press, 2015), 286.

9. Schliesser, *Sympathy*, 298.

10. Kelsey Crowe and Emily McDowell, *There Is No Good Card for This: What to Say and Do When Life Is Scary, Awful, and Unfair to People You Love* (New York: Harper One, 2017), e-book.

11. "Sympathy," Hallmark, 2004.
12. Michael Corkery and Sapna Maheshwari, "The Most Poignant Coronavirus Shortage: Selling Out of Sympathy Cards," *Chicago Tribune*, April 27, 2020, https://www .chicagotribune.com/coronavirus/ct-nw-nyt-sympathy-cards-sold-out-coronavirus -20200427-fhkhpw227fgi3e4iksyorckvku-story.html.

8: Wearing Black (Candor)

1. Lou Taylor, *Mourning Dress: A Costume and Social History* (London: George Allen & Unwin, 1983), 66.
2. Margaret M. Coffin, *Death in Early America: The History and Folklore of Customs and Superstitions of Early Medicine, Funerals, Burials, and Mourning* (Nashville: Thomas Nelson, 1976), 196.
3. Taylor, *Mourning Dress*, 65–66.
4. Dolores Monet, "History of the Mourning Dress: Black Clothing Worn during Bereavement," Bellatory, April 9, 2021, https://bellatory.com/fashion-industry /FashionHistoryMourningDressBlackClothingWornDuringBereavement.
5. Taylor, *Mourning Dress*, 124.
6. Taylor, *Mourning Dress*, 136.
7. "8 Intriguing Funeral Customs from the Victorian Era," Funeral Basics, accessed October 23, 2021, https://www.funeralbasics.org/8-intriguing-funeral-customs -victorian-era/#:~:text=For%20children%20mourning%20parents%20(or,for %20first%20cousins%2C%20four%20weeks.
8. Taylor, *Mourning Dress*, 57.
9. Coffin, *Death in Early America*, 198.
10. Lindsay Baker, "Mourning Glory: Two Centuries of Funeral Dress," BBC, November 3, 2014, https://www.bbc.com/culture/article/20141103-mourning-glory-funeral -style.
11. Woodyard, *Victorian Book of the Dead*, 101–5.
12. Baker, "Mourning Glory."
13. O'Rourke, *Long Goodbye*.
14. Chandler Lichtefeld, "Grief: Ritual Finger Amputation," Anthropological Perspectives on Death, Emory WordPress Sites, February 24, 2017, https:// scholarsblogs.emory.edu/gravematters/2017/02/24/grief-ritual-finger-amputation/.
15. Drew Gilpin Faust, *This Republic of Suffering: Death and the American Civil War* (New York: Alfred A. Knopf, 2008), 149.
16. O'Rourke, *Long Goodbye*.
17. Saran Sidime, "The Cure for Sorrow," interview with Jan Richardson, *Hidden Grief*, season 1, episode 5, August 4, 2021, https://podcasts.apple.com/us/podcast/the-cure -for-sorrow/id1554016182?i=1000530967581.
18. Katharine Doob Sakenfeld, ed., *The New Interpreter's Dictionary of the Bible*, vol. 5 (Nashville: Abingdon Press, 2009), 16.
19. David Noel Freedman, Allen C. Myers, and Astrid B. Beck, eds., *Eerdmans Dictionary of the Bible* (Grand Rapids, MI: Eerdmans, 2000), 1148.
20. Leland Ryken, James C. Wilhoit, and Tremper Longman III, eds., *Dictionary of Biblical Imagery* (Downers Grove, IL: InterVarsity Press, 2010), accessed June 4, 2021, ProQuest Ebook Central.

9: Tolling the Bell (Endurance)

1. Deborah Lubken, "How Church Bells Fell Silent: The Decline of Tower Bell Practices in Post-Revolutionary America," (2016), Publicly Accessible Penn Dissertations, https://repository.upenn.edu/edissertations/1863, page 8.

2. Lubken, "How Church Bells Fell Silent," 8.

3. Parkes and Prigerson, *Bereavement*, 124–25.

4. Puckle, *Funeral Customs*, 82–83.

5. Sam Tetrault, "What's a Death Knell? And What Happens When It Rings?" Cake, May 21, 2021. https://www.joincake.com/blog/death-knell/.

6. Smith, *To Serve the Living*, 28.

7. A. Crosby, "Death in Cades Cove," in *Appalachia: When Yesterday Is Today*, ed. Students at the University of Tennessee (Knoxville, 1965), 1–3. Quoted in Crissman, *Death and Dying in Central Appalachia*, 27.

8. This is according to https://www.etymonline.com/word/knell.

9. Elisabeth Kübler-Ross and David Kessler, *On Grief and Grieving: Finding the Meaning of Grief through the Five Stages of Loss* (New York: Scribner, 2005), 7.

10. O'Rourke, *Long Goodbye*.

11. Lubken, "How Church Bells Fell Silent," 156–57.

12. Lubken, "How Church Bells Fell Silent," 9.

13. Nicholas Wolterstorff, *Lament for a Son* (Grand Rapids, MI: Eerdmans, 1987), 5.

14. John Short, "The First Epistle to the Corinthians," in vol. 10 of *The Interpreter's Bible*, ed. George Author Buttrick, 185–86 (Nashville: Abingdon Cokesbury Press, 1953).

15. Dietrich Bonhoeffer, Reinhard Krauss and Nancy Lukens ed., *Dietrich Bonhoeffer Works*, vol. 8, *Letters and Papers from Prison* (Minneapolis: Fortress, 2009), letter no. 89, 238.

16. Parkes and Prigerson. *Bereavement*, 86–87.

17. O'Rourke, *Long Goodbye*, 184.

18. George A. Bonanno, *The Other Side of Sadness: What the New Science of Bereavement Tells Us about Life after Loss.* (New York: Basic Books, 2009), 96.

19. Mary Oliver, *Thirst: Poems* (Boston: Beacon Press, 2006), 53–54.

20. Berry, *Hannah Coulter*, 51.

10: Funeral Games (Joy)

1. Brené Brown, *The Gifts of Imperfection: Let Go of Who You Think You're Supposed to Be and Embrace Who You Are* (Center City: Hazelden Publishing, 2010).

2. Wolterstorff, *Lament for a Son*, 86.

3. Homer, *The Iliad*, trans. Robert Fagles (New York: Penguin Books 1990), 559–60.

4. Mark Golden, *Sport and Society in Ancient Greece* (Cambridge: Cambridge University Press, 1998), 92.

5. David Potter, *The Victor's Crown: A History of Ancient Sport from Homer to Byzantium* (Oxford: Oxford University Press, 2012), 30.

6. Brian O'Connell, "Lifting the Lid on Irish Wakes," *Irish Times*, March 25, 2009, accessed September 26, 2021, https://www.irishtimes.com/culture/lifting-the-lid-on-irish-wakes-1.729881.

7. Puckle, *Funeral Customs*, 62–63.

8. "Odd Games, Lewd Songs and Stories All Part of the Irish Wake," *Independent.ie*, October 13, 2012, accessed September 26, 2021, https://www.independent.ie/irish-news/odd-games-lewd-songs-and-stories-all-part-of-the-irish-wake-28G92817.html.

9. Puckle, *Funeral Customs*, 63–64.
10. "Odd Games, Lewd Songs and Stories."
11. Crissman, *Death and Dying in Central Appalachia*, 71.
12. Kevin Toolis, *My Father's Wake: How the Irish Teach Us to Live, Love, and Die* (New York: Da Capo Press, 2017), 251.
13. Melchert, *Great Conversation*, 205.
14. John Piper, "What Is Christian Hedonism?" Desiring God, August 18, 2006, https://www.desiringgod.org/interviews/what-is-christian-hedonism.
15. Kahlil Gibran, *The Prophet* (New York: Alfred A. Knopf, 1923).
16. Sittser, *Grace Disguised*, 200.
17. Sittser, *Grace Disguised*, 48.
18. Wolterstorff, *Lament for a Son*, 92.
19. Mary Oliver, *Swan: Poems and Prose Poems* (Boston: Beacon Press, 2012).

11: Death Rooms (Mortality)

1. Justin Lonas, "Where My Driveways Ends, a Cemetery Begins," *Fathom*, September 20, 2021, accessed October 8, 2021, http://www.fathommag.com/stories/where-my-driveway-ends-a-cemetery-begins.
2. Aries, *Hour of Our Death*, 29–37.
3. Aries, *Hour of Our Death*, 41.
4. Keith Eggener, interviewed by Rebecca Greenfield, "Our First Public Parks: The Forgotten History of Cemeteries," *Atlantic*, March 16, 2011, accessed October 8, 2021, https://www.google.com/amp/s/amp.theatlantic.com/amp/article/71818/.
5. Barbra Mann Wall, "History of Hospitals," Penn Nursing, University of Pennsylvania website, accessed October 6, 2021, https://www.nursing.upenn.edu/nhhc/nurses-institutions-caring/history-of-hospitals/.
6. L. S. Dugdale, *The Lost Art of Dying: Reviving Forgotten Wisdom* (New York: HarperOne, 2020), 79.
7. Dugdale, *Lost Art of Dying*, 75.
8. Faust, *This Republic of Suffering*, 92–98.
9. Gary Laderman, *Rest in Peace: A Cultural History of Death and the Funeral Home in Twentieth-Century America* (New York: Oxford University Press, 2003). 14–15.
10. Brian Walsh, "When You Die, You'll Probably Be Embalmed: Thank Abraham Lincoln for That," *Smithsonian*, November 1, 2017, accessed October 6, 2021, https://www.smithsonianmag.com/science-nature/how-lincolns-embrace-embalming-birthed-american-funeral-industry-180967038/.
11. Laderman, *Rest in Peace*, 14–15.
12. Sam Tetrault, "How Much Does the Average Funeral Cost in the US (2021 Update)," Cake, July 9, 2021, accessed October 11, 2021, https://www.joincake.com/blog/cost-of-a-funeral/.
13. Crissman, *Death and Dying in Central Appalachia*, 29–30.
14. Caroline E. Mayer, "The Slow Death of the American Living Room," *Washington Post*, August 12, 1995, accessed October 8, 2021, https://www.washingtonpost.com/archive/politics/1995/08/12/the-slow-death-of-the-american-living-room/e1cfbaae-3bee-460e-80aa-1121221ca5a3/..
15. Dugdale, *Lost Art of Dying*, 83–84.

16. Hazel Smith, "HOT DISH: The Preacher and the Song," CMT, April 22, 2005, accessed October 10, 2021, http://www.cmt.co/news/1500637/hot-dish-the -preacher-and-the-song/.

12: Decoration Day (Honor)

1. Melchert, *Great Conversation*, 204.
2. James Van Der Zee, Owen Dodson, and Camille Billops, *The Harlem Book of the Dead* (Dobbs Ferry, NY: Morgan and Morgan, 1978), 6.
3. Alan Jabbour and Karen Singer Jabbour, *Decoration Day in the Mountains: Traditions of Cemetery Decoration in the Southern Appalachians* (Chapel Hill: University of North Carolina Press, 2010), 129.
4. Crissman, *Death and Dying in Central Appalachia*, 147–52.
5. Crissman, *Death and Dying in Central Appalachia*, 152.
6. M. Ruth Little, *Sticks and Stones: Three Centuries of North Carolina Gravemarkers* (Chapel Hill: University of North Carolina Press, 1998), 3, 100.
7. Jabber and Singer Jabbour, *Decoration Day in the Mountains*, 27–28.
8. Muriel Earley Sheppard, *Cabins in the Laurel* (Chapel Hill: University of North Carolina Press, 1935, 1991), 194.
9. Jabbour and Singer Jabbour, *Decoration Day in the Mountains*, 21.
10. Jabbour and Singer Jabbour, *Decoration Day in the Mountains*, 41.
11. Earley Sheppard, *Cabin in the Laurels*, 195–96.
12. Earley Sheppard, *Cabin in the Laurels*, 129.
13. George A. Buttrick, ed., *The Interpreter's Bible: The Holy Scriptures in the King James and Revised Standard Versions* (New York: Abingdon-Cokesbury Press 1951), 280.
14. Jennifer A. Bauer, *Roan Mountain: History of an Appalachian Treasure* (Charleston, SC: History Press, 2011).

Afterword

1. Parkes and Prigerson, *Bereavement*, 82, 83, 171.
2. Rainer Maria Rilke, *Rilke's Book of Hours*, trans. Anita Barrows and Joanna Macy (New York: Riverhead Books, 2005), 45.
3. Rilke, *Rilke's Book of Hours*, 45.

About the Author

Amanda Held Opelt is an author, speaker, and songwriter. She writes about faith, grief, and creativity, and believes in the power of community, ritual, worship, and shared stories to heal even our deepest wounds. Amanda has spent fifteen years serving in the humanitarian aid sector. She lives in the mountains of Boone, North Carolina, with her husband and two young daughters.